What People Are Saying about Joan Hunter and *Power to Heal*...

We received more miracle reports when Joan Hunter was a guest on *It's Supernatural!* than from any other interview. She has much to offer in helping you receive your healing.

—Sid Roth, Host, *It's Supernatural!* TV

Joan moves in the miraculous and desires to see others changed through the power of Jesus Christ and the Holy Spirit. It is evident that her healing ministry is increasing, and you can see how the anointing of God rests upon her. She exemplifies integrity of the highest order and has a way of drawing this quality out of others. Her heart of compassion and desire to exhort is evident as she ministers to those in need.

—Marilyn Hickey, Founder and President, Marilyn Hickey Ministries

What I like about this book is that it exposes the lies of the enemy and puts health and wholeness in the right place. *Power to Heal* breaks through the theory and theology and brings practical application of God's Word to individual lives by cutting through the lies and root problems. There is tremendous freedom set forth in these practical principles.

—Rev. John G. L. Burpee, Senior Pastor, Gates of Praise, Lincoln, Nebraska, and Founder, Destiny Churches & Ministries International

Joan Hunter is a dynamic teacher, compassionate minister, and anointed healing evangelist who has devoted her life to carrying a message of hope, deliverance, and healing to the nations.

—Dr. Don White, D. D., Senior Pastor, Living Stones Church, Magnolia, Texas

We had several astounding miracles in our meetings through Joan's ministry. One of note was Nancy Vinsonhaler, who suffered abuse as a small child, the damage of which caused one arm to be three and a half inches shorter than the other. In a moment's time, the congregation audibly gasped as that section of her forearm grew those three and a half inches in a very visible, immediate miracle of God's power as Joan prayed.

—William Mark Bristow, Pastor, Grace Fellowship, Monahans, Texas

Joan Hunter helps bring us back to God's reality for our lives in *Power to Heal*. There are several intriguing chapters, but one I must encourage you to read carefully is "Don't Curse Your Blessing." The power of words can create an atmosphere that negates the manifestation of God's best. In these days when we need to overcome the world, this book is a wonderful, encouraging tool that causes faith to arise and depression to leave.

—Chuck D. Pierce, President, Glory of Zion International
Ministries, and Harvest Watchman, Global Harvest

Joan Hunter has written an excellent book on healing. It is foundational for anyone desiring God's Word to the body of Christ. It is a complete read for those needing to receive their healing, and also for those wanting to minister healing.

—Cal Pierce, International Director, Healing Rooms Ministries

Joan Hunter is a dynamic explosion of Holy Spirit power filled with compassion for others through the love of Jesus Christ. *Power to Heal* will ignite your faith, transform your life, and set you ablaze to see the miraculous works of God everywhere you go. With practical teaching, testimonies, and years of revelation, Joan Hunter's Holy Spirit-inspired words will sink deep into your heart and come alive within you to be a great witness for Christ with His power to heal. This is one book you can't put down until you've read it from cover to cover, and you won't be the same after reading it. We love this book!

—Joshua and Janet Angela Mills, Evangelists, New Wine
International, Palm Springs, California

The church today is experiencing a renewal of God's divine healing power. Joan Hunter's practical steps and scriptural prayers help ordinary believers tap into the extraordinary power of God. I recommend this book for every believer. Get ready to be launched into a new level of partnering with God and to see the miraculous release of God's healing power through your life! I highly recommend Joan Hunter's book for all who want to shift out of the ordinary and into the extraordinary life that Jesus has made available!

—Barbara Wentroble, Founder and President,
International Breakthrough Ministries

POWER
TO
HEAL

POWER
TO
HEAL

Experiencing the Miraculous

JOAN HUNTER

WHITAKER
HOUSE

Note: This book is not intended to provide medical advice or to take the place of medical advice and treatment from your personal physician. Neither the publisher, nor the author, nor the author's ministry take any responsibility for any possible consequences from any action taken by any person reading or following the information in this book. If readers are taking prescription medications, they should consult with their physicians and not take themselves off prescribed medicines without the proper supervision of a physician. Always consult your physician or other qualified health care professional before undertaking any change in your physical regimen, whether fasting, diet, medications, or exercise.

POWER TO HEAL:
Experiencing the Miraculous

ISBN: 978-1-60374-111-8
Printed in the United States of America

© 2009 by Joan Hunter
P.O. Box 1072
Pinehurst, TX 77362
www.joanhunter.org

Whitaker House
1030 Hunt Valley Circle
New Kensington, PA 15068
www.whitakerhouse.com

Library of Congress Cataloging-in-Publication Data

Hunter, Joan, 1953–
Power to heal / by Joan Hunter.
    p. cm.
    Summary: "Joan Hunter describes the path to holistic health and teaches that God can use anyone to supernaturally heal others"—Provided by publisher.
    ISBN 978-1-60374-111-8 (trade pbk. : alk. paper) 1. Spiritual healing—Christianity.
I. Title.
    BT732.5.H797 2009
    234'.131—dc22
                2009011950

3 4 5 6 7 8 9 10 **W** 15 14 13 12 11 10 09

Dedication

This book is dedicated to the ones who have lost so much, who have been hurt and abused, but who, with God's help, have made it through to health and wholeness. Some of their testimonies are in this book, and other testimonies will come through it.

This book is also dedicated to Michael David and Baby L., whom we loved with all our hearts. We thank God for allowing them into our lives, even though it was for a short time. We will see you in heaven one day.

Finally, this book is dedicated to you, the reader. Use it in your own life so that God can heal you and make you completely whole. This book will equip you to minister to others so that they can receive their wholeness, as well.

Acknowledgment

I would like to acknowledge Naida Johnson, RN, CWS, FCCWS, and ordained minister, who is my friend and dedicated editor. I have known Naida for almost three decades, and she has given her life in service to Jesus. She is one of the most selfless people I have ever known. Naida and I experienced heartache while writing this book, and yet the peace of God was with us the whole time. I believe that through our tragedies, when *we* needed healing and comforting, He was there and blessed us both through our tears. As much as this book has helped us, it is our prayer that God will bless you and heal you completely through it.

Foreword

By James W. Goll

Why another book on healing? Because we need voices of credibility and experience to arise on the scene and pave the way for the many seekers who are in desperate need. As the daughter of Charles and Frances Hunter, my friend Joan Hunter brings with her almost forty years of experience in the healing ministry. She is a person who loves the presence and power of God and is sold out to the lordship of Jesus Christ in every area of her life.

Joan not only authentically carries the miracle mantle of Jesus Christ inherited through her parents; she also carries her own calling, gifts, and anointing in a next-generation package. Joan will not only take you on the journey of how to get healed, but she will also show you how to stay healed and whole in Lord.

Want to learn about the doors that lead to illness? Want to learn how to deal with guilt, false responsibility, and forgiveness? Need a primer on salvation, being filled with the Holy Spirit, or walking in the anointing and authority of the believer? Need to learn how to shut some generational doors and receive freedom from depression? Then your search is over! These things and many more are contained in this encyclopedia of wholeness, *Power to Heal*.

As soon as you read the first paragraph of the Introduction, you will know exactly why we need this book! It comes from someone who has "been there and done that" and yet remains on a progressive journey of seeking God and saying, "More, Lord!"

It is with joy in my heart that I commend to you the writings and the anointed healing ministry of this broken and yet whole vessel. Her transparency will amaze you. The truths she shares are attainable. Many will be set free to be healed, whole, and happy to fulfill their destinies in Christ Jesus. Read and be healed!

With anticipation,

—James W. Goll
Founder of Encounters Network and Prayer Storm,
Author of *The Seer, Dream Language, Angelic Encounters*, and *The Lost Art of Intercession*

Contents

Introduction

At the time of this writing, I have been in and around the healing ministry for almost forty years. I have learned much; I have witnessed much. God has chosen to use me in ways I could only have imagined even ten years ago. I have to share—no, I am compelled to share—the things that God has shown me. Through this book, I want to impart to you at least a portion of the wisdom and revelation that God has given to me.

Within these pages, I will share the keys for you to be healed and whole. In turn, you, the reader, can share your experience and reach out to help others become whole, as well. I pray that through this book,

> ...the God of our Lord Jesus Christ, the Father of glory, may [will] give to you the [a greater] spirit of wisdom and revelation in the knowledge of Him, the eyes of your understanding being enlightened; that you may know what is the hope of His calling, what are the riches of the glory of His inheritance in the saints, and what is the exceeding greatness of His power toward us who believe, according to the working of His mighty power.   (Ephesians 1:17–19)

Read the above passage of Scripture again, and hear it as a personal prophecy to you. Accept it as a precious gift from God. You can have a greater spirit of wisdom and revelation of Him. Open your eyes to see, your ears to hear, and your heart to sense problems around you. Listen for His direction as you reach out with compassion to heal those in need.

Walk in what He has called you to do and in "*the riches of the glory of His inheritance in the saints.*" In order to receive an inheritance, someone has to die. Jesus died, so the inheritance and anointing are ours in every area of our lives. How greatly He desires that we walk in that inheritance!

Not only that, but He wants us to experience His greatness and power toward us. As you read this book, you will receive a greater wisdom and knowledge of Him.

"Where there is no vision, the people perish" (Proverbs 29:18 KJV). A dream uninterpreted is like an unopened letter from God. This is a powerful statement. Without a dream or a vision, there is no hope. God has great plans for us. We all have to accept His dream, His vision, and His plan for our lives.

Don't be afraid to dream and then see your dream come to pass. God doesn't give us dreams to motivate us and then withhold the reward like a farmer dangling a carrot in front of a donkey. He gives us dreams and visions so we can see them come to pass and then become our memories. In turn, we can dream even more. Dream your dreams. Allow them to come to pass. Share them with others. Encourage others to see their dreams come to pass. Be a willing participant in God's master plan, which is revealed to us in the Scriptures.

"Therefore do not be unwise, but understand what the will of the Lord is" (Ephesians 5:17). Pray that your eyes and ears of understanding will be totally open to His Word, and wrap your heart around the truth. Jesus still heals today—body, soul, and spirit. You are called. You are hungry. You are searching for answers. You want more of God. Read on.

Some people try to catch the wave of what God is doing; others make the wave. I want to speak to the people who are reading this: I speak this day that you are going to be a wave maker, not just one who follows others. God will raise you up to accomplish great things for Him.

It is not the number of people who read this book that matters; it is how many people go out to heal the sick through His authority after reading this book.

CHAPTER 1
Healing the Whole Man

This book is about miracles—all kinds of miracles. Do I perform the miracles? Oh, no. You don't, either. However, we are a very important and vital link in the process of the miracles that manifest around us. Without us, without our cooperation, many miracles would not occur. Years ago, I heard someone teach that Jesus is God's heart, the Holy Spirit is His mind, and we, the believers, are His hands. Without us, God can't physically "touch" others in need.

Just as He did in the Bible, Jesus Christ performs miracles today. Believers know that Jesus was a miracle worker when He walked on this earth. After He died, His Holy Spirit came to earth, enabling Him to live within us. When we accept Him into our hearts, we have the choice to allow Him to work within us and through us. Note that I said we have a choice. God gave us free will. He allows us to choose. We have the option to refuse.

It is our choice to allow Him into our hearts and lives. It is our choice to allow Him to shine forth to others through us. It is our choice to witness to the lost. It is our choice to share His love. It is our choice to accept His healing. It is our choice to allow God to use us.

If God can use me, God can use anybody. I am always amazed that God uses me, but I know God can and will use anyone who is willing. He wants everyone to fully understand that His help, His love, His power, and His healing are for everyday use. He can use you at home, at work, and anywhere else you happen to be at any moment. He will minister through you—*if* you allow Him to do it.

Allowing God to work through me is a way of life for me wherever I am—at the grocery store, in an airplane, in the airport, or at the gas station. What God does is amazing. When you realize your capability, His anointing flows, and you can lay hands on anyone, anywhere. It's so much fun!

An Introduction to Healing

Today, many of God's children are sick and looking desperately in every direction for solutions, and their Father is waiting patiently for them to finally fall to their knees and call out to Him for His divine intervention. Through the ages, there have always been a faithful few who tenaciously hung on to His promises. These few kept the Word of God alive despite the teachings of the church to the contrary; these few were miraculously healed and wouldn't keep silent. These few knew that God was the Healer.

In modern times, believing in the miraculous, healing power of God has been minimized. "Yes, it happened in Bible times, but it is not for today," they say. God hasn't changed. Jesus hasn't changed. The gifts God gave, as recorded in Scripture, are still ours today. Jesus did it all so many years ago. He paid the price. Pray that God will open your eyes to His perfect truth today, right now.

The number one answer for all our problems is Jesus. He is the one Source of healing for all disease, discomfort, and pain. He is the only "second opinion" anyone ever needs to look for or request. He knows how to cure all conditions—no matter how small or large, simple or complicated. He is the Answer.

He is the Physician, He is the Counselor, and He is the Provider. He knows the root causes of our infirmities and ailments. His healing power is not limited to the physical or mental realm. His healing goes all the way to the heart and soul of a person. He heals every aspect of your being—mental, physical, emotional, and financial. Many people consider healing to be a very complicated subject—a mysterious, unknown entity with unattainable answers hidden in impossible places.

If you depend on science, medicine, or theology for your total recovery, healing can indeed be a very long and complicated journey.

However, if you recognize the fact that there is one Person who has all the answers to any disease you have, the Answer is simple. His name is Jesus. In concert with our heavenly Father and His Holy Spirit, anyone can be healed. Jesus can heal the whole man.

Does it always take a long time? No! Is healing guaranteed? No. I can't promise or guarantee anything. Only God has that answer. After dozens of years of ministering around the world in various countries, however, I can share endless experiences of healings that I have witnessed personally, as well as documented testimonies of healings that occurred during healing schools and meetings held by my ministry.

My goal in writing this book is to share freely these keys to being healed and whole.

Healing Is Easy

It is not difficult. It is simple. We are going to get into the details of what makes healing easy and what makes it hard. Actually, we are the ones who make it hard. Through this book, we are going to break down the barriers and excuses that make it difficult for some.

That the God of our Lord Jesus Christ, the Father of glory, may give to you the spirit of wisdom and revelation in the knowledge of Him, the eyes of your understanding being enlightened; that you may know what is the hope of His calling, what are the riches of the glory of His inheritance in the saints. (Ephesians 1:17–18)

I pray that God will not only open your eyes but also your hearts to what you are capable of doing for Him. You accepted Him by faith. You accepted His love by faith. You accepted salvation by faith. After you exercised your faith, the inner knowledge of His truth and salvation, His presence within you both grew and matured. You found that you could trust Him with your heart. You may have trusted Him to care for your family members. Miraculously, the impossible started happening. Family members got saved. Barriers disappeared. Mountains were removed. Your prayers were getting answered.

You opened your heart, your mind, and your life to Him and to His will. First, you trusted Him with little things. Then, you went on to trust Him with larger things. Maybe it was the other way around. Perhaps you trusted Him only with the big things and not the little things. It is now time to take the next step and trust Him with everything, whether small or large.

Take the limits off God. We need to take the limits off ourselves, also. Even though I have been saved for many, many years, I didn't realize who I was until just a few years ago. It took some major, life-changing events before I finally opened my eyes and heart to who He wanted me to be.

Now, part of my assignment is to help you realize who you are in Christ and find the gifting He has given you. He has much more for all of us than we are walking in right now.

Choose His way and experience a whole new way of life. Allow your eyes to be enlightened to what God has for you. Don't blame the enemy. Don't give the devil credit. You chose to believe the lies that you were incapable, that you were inferior, that you were too shy, or that you didn't know enough. Now, you have heard the truth. Open your eyes and stop blaming the devil. Make the choice today.

> *And He said to them, "Go into all the world and preach the gospel to every creature. He who believes and is baptized will be saved; but he who does not believe will be condemned. And these signs will follow those who believe: In My name they will cast out demons; they will speak with new tongues; they will take up serpents; and if they drink anything deadly, it will by no means hurt them; they will lay hands on the sick, and they will recover."* (Mark 16:15–18)

Each person has a part of the assignment given to the body of Christ. God knew that one person couldn't do it all. He needs everyone to work together. He made the provision for Jesus to live within each of us and for His Holy Spirit to work through each of us. He asks us only for willing hearts and obedient spirits. He will do the rest. If you aren't seeing people healed, you aren't laying hands on the sick. However, if you can't see yourself doing it, it won't happen.

> **When you lay hands on the sick, they will recover.**

When you lay hands on the sick, they will recover. Everywhere you go, you will want to lay hands on people. If you don't lay hands on someone every day, you may feel that something isn't right—that something isn't complete for that day.

God simply needs a willing vessel. He doesn't place a list of restrictions on any person; it doesn't matter where you were born, how tall you are, how young you are, how healthy you are, how smart you are, how much education you have, or who your relatives happen to be.

God doesn't care who I am. I appreciate the fact that I am Charles and Frances Hunter's daughter. I praise God that I had the opportunity to learn from them and work with them in the ministry for all those years. But that's not why God sent me into the ministry. I'm also not in the ministry because I went to Oral Roberts University, part of another outstanding healing ministry in this country.

I am here because I'm anointed to be here. God has called me to lay hands on the sick and to see signs and wonders wherever I go. I believe God can use me. I am willing to allow Him to work through me. It is just that simple. I see miracles everywhere I go.

If you have ever been healed, no one can convince you that God does not heal. He healed me from the top of my head to the soles of my feet: physically, emotionally, mentally, and financially. Years ago, my CPA told me that I wouldn't survive another two years with my small income and three children in college. I not only made it, but God also surpassed my expectations by leaps and bounds.

Spiritually, I have always been strong because I have had to hold on to Him simply to make it through each day. Emotionally, I have been a mess. I have felt as if my heart had been dragged out of my chest, stomped on, and smashed. Jesus came along, picked up my heart, healed it, reshaped it, and gently put it back in my chest.

If God did it for me, He can do it for you. If God healed me, He can heal you. If God can heal you, He can heal anybody. The more limits you take off God, the more limits you take off yourself. You both become limitless. God wants to use you. Does He want you to go all over the world? I don't know. But He does want you to start where you are. We need to live for today. You need to be willing to go wherever God asks you to go today.

There is a difference between believing you are doing God's business and Him actually doing His business through you. Open up your heart, mind, and soul. Choose to allow Him to work in you and through you to help others.

Be the messenger, not the message.

CHAPTER 2
God Believes in Miracles

Do you believe in miracles? God does. He is the Author and Creator of all things. Some people believe He stopped doing miracles in the days of the Bible. Why would He stop? He is infinitely wise and knows all things. How can man with his finite mind make such a profound decision that God would stop performing miracles? If we believe and stand on the Scripture that says, *"Jesus Christ is the same yesterday, today, and forever"* (Hebrews 13:8), how can we not believe that He still performs miracles?

I have witnessed the birth of my two grandchildren. In my heart and soul, I believe that every birth is a true miracle from God, a very precious gift from our Father.

Why did He bring man into this world? God created man for His pleasure and glory. (See Revelation 4:11.) We are His children, and He is our loving heavenly Father. He didn't create us to cause us pain and see us suffer. He is perfect love. He wants us happy and healthy—the way He created us. It was man's downfall that brought illness and pain into our existence.

God loves us. In His compassion and mercy, He wants us to return to perfect peace. If He hadn't wanted us to return to that level, He wouldn't have sent His perfect Son as a sacrifice, as redemption for our sins to reconcile us to His side once again. Faith works by love. Because He loved His creation, He made a covenant with man through Abraham to all of his seed forever. That means every one of us can claim that inheritance and all of His blessings.

God knows our weaknesses. Jesus lived within an earthbound body for thirty-three years and felt the restrictions and limitations we face daily. Yet, in His ultimate love and compassion, He lives within believers today. He touches us in unexpected ways through His people to offer freedom and healing by His miraculous works.

Truly, the greatest miracle of all is that of salvation. Logically, to be reborn spiritually from Satan's kingdom into God's kingdom sounds impossible. But God has provided complete reconciliation so that His children can return to His side, His protection, and His love. We simply have to choose to stay under His protection and remain obedient to His Word.

Yes, God believes in miracles—and performs them every day for thousands of people around the world. They aren't as unusual as some believe. I see them all the time. Miracles are a way of life for me today. Be sensitive, keep your spiritual eyes open, and you will see them, too.

When someone needs to know why miracles happen, you can share these Scriptures with them:

God's Love

Jesus saw the huge crowd as he stepped from the boat, and he had compassion on them and healed their sick. (Matthew 14:14 NLT)

And I will establish My covenant between Me and you and your descendants after you in their generations, for an everlasting covenant, to be God to you and your descendants after you.
(Genesis 17:7)

If you then, being evil, know how to give good gifts to your children, how much more will your Father who is in heaven give good things to those who ask Him! (Matthew 7:11)

God Confirms His Promises

God made His promises to man through the covenant. Unlike man, God does not lie. (See Numbers 23:19.) Thus, He must and does fulfill His promises without exception. We can read and claim His Word. We are also free to remind Him of His Word and His promises. I have done that very thing quite often over the years. I know He has not forgotten one word He has spoken; however, I am reminding myself of His promises and increasing my faith.

In hope of eternal life which God, who cannot lie, promised before time began.... (Titus 1:2)

Who Himself bore our sins in His own body on the tree, that we, having died to sins, might live for righteousness; by whose stripes you were healed. (1 Peter 2:24)

God Wants Us Healed and Whole

And behold, a leper came and worshiped Him, saying, "Lord, if You are willing, You can make me clean." Then Jesus put out His hand and touched him, saying, "I am willing; be cleansed." Immediately his leprosy was cleansed. (Matthew 8:2–3)

When Jesus had entered Capernaum, a centurion came to Him, pleading with Him, saying, "Lord, my servant is lying at home paralyzed, dreadfully tormented." And Jesus said to him, "I will come and heal him." (Matthew 8:5–7)

Miracles Attract Souls

Just as Jesus drew the multitudes when He performed His miracles so long ago, His miracles through His servants also draw people today. When the medical community has no more answers for the ills of the world, people drop to their knees in search of God's assistance. Those who receive a miraculous healing do not quietly fade away. Everyone pays attention when someone walks out of his wheelchair, a barren woman gives birth to a miracle baby, an arm or leg grows out, a blind person sees, or a deaf-mute begins to hear and speak. Miracles attract souls searching for Him.

Then a great multitude followed Him, because they saw His signs which He performed on those who were diseased. (John 6:2)

Then His fame went throughout all Syria; and they brought to Him all sick people who were afflicted with various diseases and torments, and those who were demon-possessed, epileptics, and paralytics; and He healed them. (Matthew 4:24)

And truly Jesus did many other signs in the presence of His disciples, which are not written in this book; but these are written that you may believe that Jesus is the Christ, the Son of God, and that believing you may have life in His name. (John 20:30–31)

Jesus Fulfilled the Promises in the Word

He was wounded for our transgressions, He was bruised for our iniquities; the chastisement for our peace was upon Him, and by His stripes we are healed.

(Isaiah 53:5)

That it might be fulfilled which was spoken by Isaiah the prophet, saying: "He Himself took our infirmities and bore our sicknesses."

(Matthew 8:17)

The Prayer of Faith

The prayer of faith will save the sick, and the Lord will raise him up. And if he has committed sins, he will be forgiven. (James 5:15)

Therefore I say to you, whatever things you ask when you pray, believe that you receive them, and you will have them. (Mark 11:24)

Jesus answered and said to her, "O woman, great is your faith! Let it be to you as you desire." And her daughter was healed from that very hour. (Matthew 15:28)

He said to the woman, "Your faith has saved you. Go in peace."

(Luke 7:50)

Anointing

The power of the Lord was present to heal them.   (Luke 5:17)

The whole multitude sought to touch Him, for power went out from Him and healed them all.   (Luke 6:19)

Wherever He entered into villages, cities, or in the country, they laid the sick in the marketplaces, and begged Him that they might just touch the hem of His garment. And as many as touched Him were made well.   (Mark 6:56)

Jesus Is Alive

I am He who lives, and was dead, and behold, I am alive forevermore. Amen. And I have the keys of Hades and of Death.

(Revelation 1:18)

If you confess with your mouth the Lord Jesus and believe in your heart that God has raised Him from the dead, you will be saved.

(Romans 10:9)

His Commission and Authority Given to Believers

Most assuredly, I say to you, he who believes in Me, the works that I do he will do also; and greater works than these he will do, because I go to My Father.   (John 14:12)

He said to them, "Go into all the world and preach the gospel to every creature. He who believes and is baptized will be saved; but he who does not believe will be condemned. And these signs will follow those who believe: In My name they will cast out demons; they will speak with new tongues; they will take up serpents; and if they drink anything deadly, it will by no means hurt them; they will lay hands on the sick, and they will recover." (Mark 16:15–18)

When He had called His twelve disciples to Him, He gave them power over unclean spirits, to cast them out, and to heal all kinds of sickness and all kinds of disease.... "And as you go, preach, saying, 'The kingdom of heaven is at hand.' Heal the sick, cleanse the lepers, raise the dead, cast out demons. Freely you have received, freely give." (Matthew 10:1, 7–8)

Harvest from a Planted Seed

Blessed is he who considers the poor; the LORD *will deliver him in time of trouble. The* LORD *will preserve him and keep him alive, and he will be blessed on the earth; You will not deliver him to the will of his enemies. The* LORD *will strengthen him on his bed of illness; You will sustain him on his sickbed.* (Psalm 41:1–3)

Chosen by God

You did not choose Me, but I chose you and appointed you that you should go and bear fruit, and that your fruit should remain, that whatever you ask the Father in My name He may give you.
(John 15:16)

For His Glory

The multitude marveled when they saw the mute speaking, the maimed made whole, the lame walking, and the blind seeing; and they glorified the God of Israel. (Matthew 15:31)

Freedom from the Curse of the Law

Christ has redeemed us from the curse of the law, having become a curse for us (for it is written, "Cursed is everyone who hangs on a tree"), that the blessing of Abraham might come upon the Gentiles in Christ Jesus, that we might receive the promise of the Spirit through faith.   (Galatians 3:13–14)

To Thwart the Enemy

God anointed Jesus of Nazareth with the Holy Spirit and with power, who went about doing good and healing all who were oppressed by the devil, for God was with Him.   (Acts 10:38)

He who sins is of the devil, for the devil has sinned from the beginning. For this purpose the Son of God was manifested, that He might destroy the works of the devil.   (1 John 3:8)

Obedience to His Word

If you diligently heed the voice of the LORD your God and do what is right in His sight, give ear to His commandments and keep all His statutes, I will put none of the diseases on you which I have brought on the Egyptians. For I am the LORD who heals you.
                                              (Exodus 15:26)

Gifts of the Spirit

To another [is given] faith by the same Spirit, to another gifts of healings by the same Spirit, to another the working of miracles....
                                       (1 Corinthians 12:9–10)

The Name of Jesus

Then Peter said, "Silver and gold I do not have, but what I do have I give you: In the name of Jesus Christ of Nazareth, rise up and walk."   (Acts 3:6)

His name, through faith in His name, has made this man strong, whom you see and know. Yes, the faith which comes through Him has given him this perfect soundness in the presence of you all.

(Acts 3:16)

The Power of the Holy Spirit

If the Spirit of Him who raised Jesus from the dead dwells in you, He who raised Christ from the dead will also give life to your mortal bodies through His Spirit who dwells in you. (Romans 8:11)

These Scriptures and others show you not only God's love but also His willingness and ability to heal you—and not only to heal you, but also to work through you to heal others. They also show you that He doesn't use only one way to achieve His purposes. He works in many ways to prove His Word is true.

We have to believe in Him and His Word. Yes, there are other things that affect miracles and healings in our lives. For instance, both our words and our actions can affect our futures. Some are things we are to do; some are things we are not to do. Read through those verses again—some of them have conditions attached to His promises. If and when we walk in obedience to Him, exciting miracles will happen.

CHAPTER 3

Am I Qualified?

Who am I that God would use me? Out of all the people around the world, why did God choose me?

Not only did He choose me, but I also had to choose to follow Him in what He called me to do. There are two sides to every situation. Someone calls; someone else has to answer. Someone chooses a relationship; the other person has to choose to respond.

Often, we might not understand what God's purpose is when He asks us to do something for Him. In faith, we must choose to trust Him and follow His directions.

Several years ago, I spoke at a Teen Challenge for the first time. I asked myself, *What do I have to offer these people? I have never done drugs. I have never drunk alcohol. I have never been in prison. Some of them have been suicidal. What can I tell them when I have never done or experienced any of those things?*

While I was sharing with them, God said to me, "You may not have been in prison like they have, but you were imprisoned in your mind through the years when you did not know who you were." I had lived in the shadow of being Charles and Frances Hunter's daughter. Also, negative comments from my teachers frequently popped up to remind me of my inadequacies. I was often told that I was dumb, ignorant, or retarded. For all those years, I had chosen to listen to the fears of my past rather than to what God had to say about me.

God changed things through the years. In 1971, I received excellent results on an IQ test. The first person I called was my brother (who has always been brilliant). I told him that, according to the world's standards, I wasn't retarded—I just learned differently than the average person.

There are many things that keep us from being used of God, such as the past, gender, previous poor choices, lack of experience, or insufficient training. It dawned on me that many of us have been trapped in a form of prison—whether physical or mental—for many, many years.

I asked those at Teen Challenge, "How many of you need to forgive your fathers?" Grown men and women started crying uncontrollably. Through our ministry that day, many people became totally free from unforgiveness, rejection, and the spirit of suicide.

God chose me because of my willingness and my heart for Him, not because of my past, my education, or who my parents are. He called me, and I accepted. I was and am willing to be used of God. God is looking for willing people He can use, based not on their pasts but on their futures and their willingness to die to themselves and sacrifice whatever it takes to get the job done.

You Are Who God Says You Are

When I first started traveling on the road with my parents, I didn't know who I was. If it was a choice between my mom and dad, with their worldwide healing ministry, or me, their inexperienced daughter, whom would you ask to pray for you? I imagined all the people saying, "Who does she think she is that she can pray for me?"

My insecure thoughts caused inferior feelings and responses in many areas of my life. I suffered from low self-esteem to begin with, and when I found myself on the road with Mom and Dad, my insecurities exploded. People expected me to be a younger Frances Hunter, not Joan.

When I traveled with them, I would look for the deepest, darkest, tallest, thickest, blackest curtain to hide behind. Mom would find me— perhaps by a word of knowledge. She would pull me out of my comfort zone and make me go out to greet the people. She would take my arm and force me out against all of my wishes. I dug my heels into the ground, but she would still push me out among the people.

I did get mad, but today, I am grateful for what she did. By being forced out of my comfort zone, I slowly learned that I could follow her example and minister to others. God has freed me in that area, just like He wants to free you. God wants you out of the corner. He doesn't necessarily want to put you on a platform, but He wants you to be willing and accessible to others so that they can be healed through you. When God has called you, you don't have to answer to people who say, "God can't use you because you used to do this, that, or the other."

I used to battle similar comments directed at me. Unfortunately, I had to go through a divorce. I didn't choose to be in that situation or to endure that life. Unfortunately, my divorce was the direct result of marital unfaithfulness on the part of my first husband. It was a long, painful process, but the decision to divorce was made by searching the Scriptures (see Matthew 5:32; 19:9) and realizing that it was the right thing to do.

People didn't believe that God could use me because I was a divorced woman. People marked me. I faced that situation every day and often fell to my knees. After believing for many years that my first husband would be delivered and set free according to the Word of God, I finally had to face the fact that he had made the choice not to repent or change. I was forced into a divorce. I could no longer live in that situation.

My present husband is a wonderful man, a blessing whom God has sent to me as part of my restoration package. God promises to restore what the enemy has stolen, and He has not only restored it but multiplied it back. I thank God numerous times each day for my husband, Kelley Murrell.

The Word does not say that God cannot use a divorced person. The Word of God says you can repent of any sin in your life. When repentance is placed upon the cross under the blood of Jesus Christ, you are made whiter than snow. I don't know how that works. You can be dark and full of sin, get doused with red blood, and come out white. It doesn't make sense, but the things of God don't always make sense to man's logical mind. For example, if you give, you'll have more. That doesn't make sense to the world, but that is just how God is. According to the world, if you give, you are going to have less; but with God, when you give, you will have more. With God, dark sin plus the red blood of Christ equals white. That is just the way it is.

Years ago, I would often go back to my hotel room dejected and frustrated. I knew that I knew that I knew that God had called me and was working through me, but the words of man were contradicting God. People sent letters to my parents and to me, saying I was a hypocrite and claiming that God couldn't use me because I had been divorced.

I cried out to my heavenly Father, "God, just look at what they are saying. What about the blind eye? What about the deaf ear? They can see and hear now. What about the back that got healed? What about this one or that one? Some people said You couldn't use me, but all those people got healed tonight."

> **Then, He spoke to me through His Holy Spirit and said, "Just remember, they are not the ones who called you; I am!"**

Then, He spoke to me through His Holy Spirit and said, "Just remember, they are not the ones who called you; I am!"

I quickly replied, "Yes, Sir." I no longer allowed those letters or phone calls bother me. I don't have to answer to those people. I have to answer to God alone for fulfilling His call on my life. Someone else's opinion of me doesn't have to become my reality! I believe my Father, and that's what is important.

If people ever doubt that God can use you because of your past, they are denying the power of the blood of Jesus Christ in your life and the power of forgiveness where sin is concerned. Always, always remember that. You must also understand that the biggest Goliath you will ever face in your life is the one you see in the mirror every morning.

All around the world, I have asked people, "Who will keep you from praying for the sick?" The number one response is, "The devil!" Sorry, the devil cannot keep you from praying for the sick; however, your flesh can. Do not give the devil the credit for what you are doing. He doesn't deserve it.

No matter what problem might be keeping you from being used by God—whether it is sin in your life, a physical or emotional difficulty, a social or relationship issue, or a financial crisis—remember that God is not limited by your circumstances. The next time you feel that God can't use you, just remember:

- Noah drank too much.
- Abraham was too old.
- Jacob was a liar.
- Leah was ugly.
- Joseph was abused.
- Moses had a speech problem.
- Gideon was afraid.
- Samson was a womanizer.
- Rahab was a prostitute.
- Jeremiah was too young.
- Timothy had a weak stomach.
- David had an affair and was a murderer.
- Elijah was suicidal.
- Jonah ran from God.
- Naomi was a widow.
- Job went bankrupt.
- Peter denied Christ.
- The disciples fell asleep while praying.
- Martha worried about everything.
- The Samaritan woman was divorced more than once.
- Zacchaeus was too small.
- And Lazarus was dead.

This list represents some of the people God chose to use in the Bible. The only One who is not on the list is Jesus. He is our perfect Example. We are to be His reflection. We are each to be a representative of Christ on earth as He works in and through us, based on the Word of God.

The accounts of these people in the Bible let us know that God uses imperfect people to accomplish His will. I want to be one of the people He can use. I don't claim to be perfect. I strive to be all that I can be, to do all that I can do for God, to live a clean life, and to serve Him with all of my heart. But I'm still not perfect.

Understand that God has called you for a specific purpose in life. You are not called based on who your earthly parents are. You are called because of who your heavenly Father is.

Many people fall into one of the categories on "the list." David had an affair with a married woman, found out who her husband was, and had him killed. Even though David became a murderer, he also became one of the greatest kings of history, as well as *a man after* [God's] *own heart*" (1 Samuel 13:14). Through his lineage came Jesus. As a result of repentance, and instead of condemnation for his sin, David gained everlasting life through reconciliation with his heavenly Father.

Let's use a simple cigarette lighter to compare the insignificant power of Satan to the magnificent power of God. The small flame from the lighter represents the power of Satan. Our God is the sun. Any questions? The enemy's small flame is easily snuffed out, while God shines brightly forever. In this analogy, man is represented by the moon, which reflects the sun. We are to reflect God's Son! Think about it a minute. Who is in charge? Who is in control? Whom should we answer to?

Now, you have to choose. Who is in control of your life? Are you going to hide, or will you step out with faith to help others? Let me encourage you with the voice of experience. Allowing God to control your steps is so much better and so much more fun. We were designed by Him for His pleasure. When we willingly place ourselves totally in His hands, we are in His perfect will. His perfect joy and peace take over, and I can't find words to describe that experience.

Get out of your comfort zone whenever He directs you to reach out to others. Allow Him to work through you. Let God use you. It is better to be prepared for an opportunity that doesn't occur than to be unprepared when an opportunity to be used by God arises.

The enemy doesn't even have to worry about lying or deceiving you as long as you're believing the negative about yourself. Don't give in to the flesh and convince yourself that God can't use you or heal through you.

Remember, we have the mind of Christ. He is actually living through us. We can plug into more than just His mind—we can plug into His heart. He can love through us, and He can heal through us. Just ask yourself that common question: "What would Jesus do?" *"Let this mind be in you which was also in Christ Jesus"* (Philippians 2:5).

Become Who He Wants You to Be

As Jesus left the house, he was followed by two blind men crying out, "Mercy, Son of David! Mercy on us!" When Jesus got home, the blind men went in with him. Jesus said to them, "Do you really believe I can do this?" They said, "Why, yes, Master!" He touched their eyes and said, "Become what you believe." It happened. They saw.
(Matthew 9:27–30 MSG)

Up until this day, you have become what you have believed because of what others have told you, because of what you have done and accomplished. This book is about changing what you believe about yourself, expanding your expectations of God and of yourself. After reading this book, what you believe about yourself and your potential will change. Are you ready?

As I was sharing this one day, God spoke to me, saying, "Tell them that I have become what they believe."

Think about that. Can you grasp the power in that statement? If you believe He is Love, He is. If you believe He is the Healer, He is. If you believe He can and will work through you, He will!

We can do what we believe we can do. We can become what we believe we can become. We are limited by our belief in ourselves. With

35

the help of God, you can change your limited beliefs and raise your level of expectation. Change is an integral part of life. Nothing stays the same forever—except God. However, He can and will change us. Sometimes, the changes are surprising and unusual, but they are not impossible.

For instance, when the word *watermelon* is mentioned, we all visualize the large, green, rounded fruit we find at the supermarket during the summer. Watermelons don't fit easily into the refrigerator, and they roll if they are bumped. They are usually piled in large bins at the store because of their awkward shapes and sizes.

Someone in Japan decided to try something different. While a watermelon was small and still growing, he placed it within a square frame. Instead of becoming its usual rounded shape, it developed into a square. In this new shape, it could be stored easily, and it no longer rolled away. Its shape had conformed to the desire of the developer. Today, these watermelons are sold all over Japan. It is still the delicious fruit we know and love, but its shape catches your attention.

God can use each of us. He wants us to serve Him by sharing His message with others who need Him and His healing power. Allowing God to work through you will be a silent but earth-shattering testimony to the people around you. Often, what you do speaks louder than what you say. Become what God wants you to be.

Do What He Wants You to Do

A lady in south Texas was diagnosed as being legally blind. She was concerned about her situation because she wanted to be used by God. She felt that her condition limited her ability to reach others. She prayed. One day, she went to her husband with an urgent request. "Please, take me to the mall. There is someone there I have to pray for." He drove her to the mall and led her down the center aisle until she suddenly stopped in front of a lady sitting on a bench.

This obedient, legally blind believer listened to God's voice and, at just the right time, was led to the exact place to minister to someone in need. She said, "God sent me to the mall to pray for you today. What do you need Him to do?"

Indeed, the lady had been praying for an answer to a problem. The lady looked up from where she was sitting and said, "When I got up this morning, I told God, 'If You are real, send somebody to the mall today to tell me.'"

Since that day, the blind woman's vision has improved. She can travel on her own without assistance. God has rewarded her obedience.

I want you to be a person whom God uses!

> **I want you to be a person whom God uses!**

A gentleman was accidentally electrocuted many years ago. His hands were irreparably burned. Did this roadblock stop him? No. He doesn't have hands to lay on people, but when he lays his prosthetic hooks on people, they get dramatically healed.

Now, I have to ask you: What is holding you back from ministering to others?

Prayer of Repentance

Father, I have sinned. I repent of the sin of disobedience and of not doing everything You have called me to do in walking out Your call on my life. Take this sin. Put it on the cross. On the day of judgment, hold no accusations against me. Father, bless me. Holy Spirit, guide and help me. I willingly choose to walk with You, talk with You, and follow Your direction to the best of my ability from this day forth. Help me to stay within Your perfect will and reach out to others who need to see You and know You. Change my belief in myself. Let me become who You believe I can be. In Jesus' name, amen.

Repentance is very powerful in every area of our lives.

CHAPTER 4
Authority of the Believer

All believers are commissioned by Jesus. He had the God-given authority to lay hands on the sick and see them recover. In turn, He gave His authority to His followers. Before He went back to heaven, He gave the Great Commission to all of us—not just the people who were present at the time. Through the Great Commission, we now have His authority available to us. We, as believers, must receive and use that authority, but few of us understand the importance or usage of that authority.

A friend of mine is in the security business. When he was assigned to protect some princes from a foreign country, he had to go into places of the world that he would never have chosen to go unless it was a requirement of his job. While working on this assignment, he learned a lot about God.

The princes knew who they were. They were sons of a king. They held their heads high and threw their shoulders back. They represented their father, their king. They knew their authority because of what the king had given them. They knew they had all the finances they would ever need in their lifetimes. They didn't have to worry about security because they had professional bodyguards ensuring their safety at all times. They did not worry about who they were because they knew they were children of a king. They walked in total confidence, not pride.

What can a person learn in the midst of all that worldly activity? We are not just children of a king, we are children of *the* King of kings. We have to know who our Father is and what our responsibilities are as His children. We can walk in His authority.

God's Promises to His Children

What has God promised to His children? What does He expect of His children? In other words, do you know who you are? Do you know

38

what God wants from you? Do you understand that He can use you? Do you know and understand His authority?

When you eat a filling meal, such as a roast, the food will keep you satisfied for a long time. Occasionally, however, you might eat something that goes right through your digestive system and gives you little nutritional value, such as broth. Our use of God's Word can be viewed in the same manner. We are to take in and absorb the Word, not just rush through it like we would a quick snack. Allow God's Word to accomplish the purpose for which it was intended.

Let's find out what the Word says about our authority.

Jesus called his twelve disciples together and gave them authority to cast out evil spirits and to heal every kind of disease and illness.
(Matthew 10:1 NLT)

I have given you authority over all the power of the enemy, and you can walk among snakes and scorpions and crush them. Nothing will injure you. But don't rejoice because evil spirits obey you; rejoice because your names are registered in heaven. (Luke 10:19–20 NLT)

Most assuredly, I say to you, he who believes in Me, the works that I do he will do also; and greater works than these he will do, because I go to My Father. And whatever you ask in My name, that I will do, that the Father may be glorified in the Son. If you ask anything in My name, I will do it. (John 14:12–14)

Most people know that God can heal, but they don't believe that God will use them to do it. Mark 16:17–18 says that those who believe are going to cast out devils and lay their hands on the sick, and the sick are going to be healed.

When you understand that God wants to heal you and heal through you, you will be totally and completely transformed. You will know that Jesus Christ has given His authority to each of us. He has deposited much into our accounts. We need to appropriate what He has deposited within us and use it as He intended. We don't need to run around, pray for days on end, or work ourselves into a fervor to use His anointing or authority.

Several years ago, a pastor asked a lady to minister with me. I didn't know her. When I saw her for the first time, she was in the front of the church, going, "*Rrrrnnnddd!*" over and over again.

"Excuse me, what are you doing?" I asked.

She replied, "I'm mustering up the anointing."

No mustering is necessary! You don't have to warm up your hands. You don't have to run around the platform. Understand that the anointing goes everywhere with you and is available at all times.

God Has Given Us the Authority

Once, before I spoke at a breakfast meeting, I went into the restroom to get ready. A lady walked into the restroom and said, "Wow! The anointing is so strong in here."

My thought was, *That's an unusual statement.* However, you must understand that the anointing and His authority go with you wherever you are, whether you are in the bathroom, at the grocery store, or in the pulpit. If someone in the restroom needs healing, she doesn't have to go to a service or to church. Jesus can heal in the restroom. The anointing flows in and through you wherever you go.

If you are willing to give God a few seconds, He will use you wherever you go.

If you find a person who needs healing, don't tell him, "Wait just a minute" while you start speaking in tongues. When you turn back to pray, he will be gone. You must be ready in season and out. If someone who is sick asks for your help, you need to be ready to lay hands on him right where you are, whether in the marketplace, at work, or elsewhere.

Did you say, "I don't have time to pray for someone on my job"? All you have to say is, "In the name of Jesus, I speak a new pancreas [or whatever needs to be healed] into this body. Thank You, Jesus!" You always have at least that much time, wherever you might be. If you are willing to give God those few seconds, God will use you wherever you go.

Healing can occur in many ways. First and most important, pray in Jesus' name. You can lay hands on the sick, you can pray over the phone, or you can send a prayer over the Internet—*in Jesus' name*. I recently sent a healing prayer text message to a friend who had gotten very ill while visiting another country. She texted me back a few minutes later, saying that she had been healed and was able to get on a plane to come home.

God has given us the authority, and we, in turn, can speak the Word and heal those in need, whether through a phone call, an e-mail, or in person. It is awesome. Don't limit God or how He can use you.

Is it necessary to know all the details of the problems or disease? No, you don't need the history of what, how, or why things have happened; however, I personally feel that the more specific your prayers are, the greater the results will be.

When my children were growing up (I have four grown daughters), I would often call into the next room, "I need someone to vacuum the living room." Guess what? No one would respond. I would then say, "Charity, I need the living room vacuumed." Charity would get up and vacuum the living room. Because I was specific, because I called Charity by name, she moved from where she was and completed her assignment. When we call a disease by a specific name as we minister, the Word of God more readily accomplishes what it is meant to do.

The disease is commanded to *go*, and the new part is commanded to *enter*. Diseases are healed, old body parts are replaced, and health is restored. These wonderful, glorious miracles occur so often that I can't even count them anymore. It is marvelous. It is Jesus.

The president of the United States has authority in our government, but he has to use it. You have been given all the authority of Jesus Christ, but it's up to you to use it. You can choose to use it or let it lie dormant. When you know that the God-given authority of Jesus Christ lives in and through you, you can lay hands on the sick with confidence. I am using it to the fullest extent possible—*in Jesus' name.*

Healing is logical—don't make it harder than it is. If a person has problems with his heart but doesn't know the specific details, what do you pray? "In the name of Jesus, I speak in a new heart." Don't make it harder than it is. We have had testimonies from many people who have returned to very busy lifestyles because they received new hearts. Some have been taken off the transplant list. Praying "in the name of Jesus" works; however, the percentage of people healed without elaborating further in prayer is minimal. I would rather go for 95 percent than for 3 percent. The more specific you can be when you pray, the more specific the results will be.

Avenues to Healing

Basking in His presence, listening to teaching and music CDs or DVDs, and worshipping the Lord can also bring healing to a hurting body. Part of this experience reduces stress and replaces negative behavior with God's healing presence. His presence in the music and teaching will prepare a person's heart for healing.

Miracle services have an enhanced atmosphere of healing. A combination of intercession, expectation, worship, teaching, and individual prayer all contribute to the healing process. The atmosphere gets thick with miracles. I can be praying for someone's back in one area of the service, and someone on the other side of the room will receive her healing. God's healing flows throughout the auditorium, touching people who just bask in His presence.

Even when you are praying alone, God agrees with you if you are praying according to His Word.

The Word of God says, *"If two of you agree on earth concerning anything that they ask, it will be done for them by My Father in heaven"* (Matthew 18:19). Where two or more are gathered in agreement, miracles can happen. Remember, even when you are praying alone, God agrees with you if you are praying according to His Word. The prayer of agreement is a powerful tool when healing is needed.

If you have been in a large meeting of believers or have watched a meeting on television, you have probably seen or heard a *word of knowledge* being given from the platform. This is one of the gifts of the Spirit; a word of knowledge can be spoken, and a person will be healed. Often, in very large crowds, the word is accepted, claimed, and believed by more than one person. They all get healed. A word of knowledge can also be given in private. Basically, the Holy Spirit will give you knowledge about someone, something, or some place that you would not have known about in any other way.

Can the healing anointing be transferred to inanimate objects? One of the most common methods is the use of prayer cloths. Easy to obtain and share, a small piece of cloth that has been prayed over or been close to an anointed person can have spiritual effects on another person who carries it.

Several women I know have quietly placed prayer cloths in the pillows of their unsaved husbands. Another friend placed one in her checkbook for extra anointing on her finances. The book of Acts tells us that when pieces of Paul's clothing were laid on people, the sick were healed. Just like many other ministries, we send thousands of prayer cloths around the world. Testimonies of restorations of all kinds come in regularly.

Anointing with oil is also a well-known method of healing. Whether administered by the elders of the church or simply given from believer to believer, anointing with oil is a powerful practice.

So they went out and preached that people should repent. And they cast out many demons, and anointed with oil many who were sick, and healed them. (Mark 6:12–13)

Calling for the elders of the church to do the anointing with oil is very common. The term *elders* covers all the mature believers who freely pray for the sick or those in need. They pray the prayer of faith, and people are healed. This tells us that the pastors and other leaders of the church are not the only ones who can pray in faith for others and anoint them with oil.

If you are in the presence of anointed people, their anointing will radiate out to others around them. People often report that they are healed by just coming to the platform. The closer they get to me, the heavier the anointing, so more healings happen. Sometimes, the degree of healing can be related to the amount of need or expectation of the person coming for healing. I have often said, "Get your expectors up!" Expect God to do something. Know that He will heal you. Seek in faith. Reach out to lay hands on others with equal expectation that God will work through you.

Years ago, when my parents were still traveling, my dad would have people stand so that his shadow would be cast upon them. As my dad walked by, his shadow would pass over them, and they would be completely healed. You may think this is strange, but it is quite scriptural. When Peter's shadow passed over the sick, they were healed.

Believers were increasingly added to the Lord, multitudes of both men and women, so that they brought the sick out into the streets and laid them on beds and couches, that at least the shadow of Peter passing by might fall on some of them. Also a multitude gathered from the surrounding cities to Jerusalem, bringing sick people and those who were tormented by unclean spirits, and they were all healed.

(Acts 5:14–16)

Don't limit yourself to just one way of healing. The suggestions listed here are not the only methods by which God heals. These guidelines are to help you get up and going. Listen to God. Heed His Spirit. Minister in the way He tells you to minister. I don't advocate spitting on the ground and putting mud on someone's eyes like Jesus did in the Bible; however, He can work through many mysterious ways, as well as through unsuspecting people, to accomplish His perfect will.

A certain couple has worked in the ministry for years. Their grandson heard this message on healing when he was ten years old. If the children who attend his public school get sick, they are sent to him for prayer. If a teacher is sick, she seeks him out for healing prayer. Through a young boy willing to stand up for Jesus, prayer is spreading through his public school.

What You Forget Can't Change Your Life

Ephesians 1:17–19 and Mark 16 are quoted often during my teachings. Why? Because what you forget can't change your life. I don't want you to forget anything. I want everyone to be transformed and changed by the power of God, having a spirit renewed by His authority and power. We have much work to do.

When you pray for people, you may often think, *What if they don't get healed?* That thought is not from God; the devil isn't putting that thought into your head, either. You are thinking it to yourself because you doubt that God can really use you. Get rid of that thought. Kill that Goliath in the mirror.

It is not your responsibility for the person to be healed. It *is* your responsibility to lay hands on the sick and pray. Get on with life and say, "No, lying devil, no negative thought of mine is going to keep me from laying hands on the sick wherever I go. I have the mind of Christ. That thought would never enter His mind, and therefore, it shouldn't enter mine, either!"

Christ knew beyond a shadow of a doubt that God was going to heal in and through Him. You need to know beyond a shadow of a doubt that God can heal in and through you. If I pray for someone and he is not healed, I am shocked—not the other way around.

One or two hundred people may be healed during a meeting. One may not. We

It is not your responsibility for the person to be healed. It is your responsibility to lay hands on the sick and pray.

45

will go on with additional ministry and deal with root causes, such as bitterness, resentment, unholy covenants, unforgiveness, and curses. Everyone will eventually get healed throughout the series of meetings.

Don't use the phrase, "Father, if it be Your will...." It *is* God's will to heal every person. Jesus took thirty-nine stripes on His back for my healing. He took thirty-nine stripes on His back for your healing. He's not going to say, "I am going to heal only 20 percent of the people." Jesus went around healing *all* who were sick and oppressed. (See Acts 10:38.) *All* includes *everything* and excludes *nothing*—not one person!

You must know the authority of Jesus Christ and understand that you walk in that authority.

A lady came to me whispering a request for prayer for her children. I looked at her and said, "These are your two children who need prayer. I need to hear your 'mommy voice'."

Let me explain. A mother has authority over her children. If she is trying to get them to stop doing something that might hurt them, she's not going to whisper an order to them or pray quietly in a corner; she will know and speak with authority as a mother. Her son will know she is serious when he hears, "Tommy, stop that right now!" He knows that he must obey that voice of authority.

The lady repeated her request using a firm voice of authority as a mother: "My children need prayer for...."

And I thought, *Yes! There is the voice of authority!* Screaming and yelling until you lose your voice is not necessary. Even a mother's whisper *with* authority will motivate a child. Even in public places where quietness is expected, such as airplanes, you can pray for someone very quietly but still *with authority*. People get healed on planes all the time.

Whispering, "Well, God, it would be nice if You healed..." is not praying with authority. It is not the volume that counts; it is *knowing* your authority in the name of Jesus. You can whisper or you can yell as loudly as you want. "In the name of Jesus, I command that stinking, lousy cancer to leave. It is cursed, and I command it to dry up in the name of Jesus."

However, if you are in a public place, whether in a supermarket, at an airport, or at work, you don't need to call attention to yourself or the person for whom you are praying. You can simply smile and say quietly, "Thank You, Jesus!" Screaming and jumping around may scare or embarrass the person for whom you are praying, as well as others nearby.

During an interview on a television show, the host of the program asked me, "What do you do in the marketplace? How do you handle that?" I replied, "When I pray for someone in the marketplace, the person for whom I am praying and I are the only ones who know I am praying."

The Word says, *"Watch and pray"* (Matthew 26:41). So, I say, "Watch as I pray." I know that Jesus prayed with His eyes open. How do I know that? How could He know the disciples fell asleep while He was praying unless He saw them fall asleep? He prayed with open eyes. I am not saying that it's wrong to close your eyes while you are praying, because sometimes you need to remove distractions. However, when you are praying for someone, keep your eyes open.

I will start by asking, "May I pray for you today?" When she agrees, I will say, "I just want you to know that only you and I will know that I am praying for you." I will smile like I'm having a pleasant, normal conversation as I continue, "Father, in the name of Jesus, I just speak a whole new knee into her, in Jesus' name, and I command all the pain to go away."

Suddenly, she gets a whole new knee, the pain goes away, and she smiles and continues her work without her fellow employees knowing that I prayed. None of the other customers know that I have prayed. Without any fanfare, she just got healed. She didn't really know who I was, either. She just knew that God touched her.

There is nothing in the Word of God that says you must pray religiously with fancy words or voice. You need to act and speak with the authority of

You are a child of the King. Act like it!

Jesus Christ, lay hands on the sick, and watch them recover. Take the healing power of God beyond the four walls of the church and to the four corners of the earth—into the marketplace, the grocery store, your job, and especially into your home. Take it wherever you go. Walk and act in authority. You are a child of the King. Act like it!

A man in Guatemala had to shut down his healing ministry because nobody was getting healed. A few years later, he heard that I was coming to Guatemala to do a healing school training session. While he attended the two-day session to discover what he could learn, his knees were healed. When he returned home, his daughter asked him, "What have you been doing?"

He replied, "I went to hear this American evangelist who trains others to pray for the sick."

She said, "Really? I have this pain in my neck. Would you pray for it?" Just as he had learned to do during the teaching session, he had her extend her arms in front of her, and then he prayed. Her arm grew out, and her neck was totally healed. At that point, the daughter said, "Dad, my best friend's mom is very sick with stage IV cancer. Would you go and pray for her?"

He agreed and went to the lady's house, where she was completely bedridden. He prayed exactly as he had learned to during the training session. From previous teaching, he felt that he was supposed to cry, read the Bible, and speak in tongues, but he didn't do those things.

It's not wrong to do those things, but doing them will not make someone get healed. The Word of God says that we are to lay hands on the sick and they will recover. (See Mark 16:18.) Their healing is based on the authority of Jesus Christ and His name, not on how hard we cry or how many Scriptures we speak over them.

This man thought, *I have done everything this book tells me to do; I haven't done any of the things I was taught before. Oh, well!* He closed the book, told the lady good-bye, and went home.

The following week, he decided to go back to pray for the lady the "right" way—the way he had been taught previously. He arrived at the house and asked for the lady. Her daughter said, "I'm sorry, you just missed her."

He was extremely saddened, thinking he hadn't gotten there before she had died. The daughter quickly said, "Don't be upset. She's just out running errands."

This man is now back in full-time healing ministry. He is excited because he has found out how to appropriate the power of God through the authority of Jesus Christ, and now he can watch miracles happen.

One pastor explained, "I'm tired of seeing people sick in my church. I want to see them well. I gave them all copies of your book several months ago. Since then, we have had only a handful of sick people. We had to invite outsiders to have a miracle service because no one in this church was sick." This pastor caught the vision and acted on it.

God is not looking for your ability; He is looking for your availability. He is not looking for superstars; He is looking for servants. Does the Scripture say, *"Well done, good and faithful superstar"*? No, it says, *"Well done, good and faithful servant"* (Matthew 25:23).

As God's children and servants, we are not functioning or working for or by ourselves. We are successful only by plugging into and working with His authority. Knowing our authority in Him, we obediently allow Him to use our bodies, minds, and spirits to accomplish His plan on earth.

God is not looking for your ability; He is looking for your availability.

Are you willing? I am!

CHAPTER 5

What Opens the Door to Illness

The true cause of illness is sometimes obscure, even to those in the medical profession. Doctors run tests and tell you that a part of your body is no longer working properly; however, giving you the reason or cause for the malady is sometimes beyond even their capable hands and medical knowledge. God has revealed to many of His servants the root causes of numerous illnesses. This is not a new concept, as you will soon discover.

> **When you walk in the sin of disobedience, you are opening the door for sickness to enter your body.**

In the next few chapters, we will cover word curses, bitterness, unforgiveness, stress, guilt, and resentment. All of these things can bring sickness into our lives. One fact that is very important to recognize up front is that sin can open the door to sickness. Sin gives the devil permission to attack your body with sickness. When you walk in the sin of disobedience, you are opening the door for sickness to enter your body.

We all have heard and know that we must follow the Ten Commandments. Many of us can honestly say we follow the "Big Ten" to the best of our abilities. We are holding God in utmost reverence and worship. We are honoring our parents and not desiring another's spouse. We aren't killing or stealing. We are even doing our best to follow Jesus' command to love others as we love ourselves. (See Matthew 22:39.)

Some may ask, "Isn't that all we have to do?" If you want to slide into heaven after fighting a bumpy life, you can indeed stop there. The big question is: Do you want *all* God has to offer?

Salvation is vitally important to each of us, but salvation is like the first rung of the ladder—the kindergarten of what God intends for His beloved children. Are you hungry for more? Are you searching for God's ultimate best for your life and for the lives of those you love?

God didn't choose me to "tickle" anyone's ears, even though my ministry is based on love, compassion, and healing. To reach the ultimate in any area takes work, study, and understanding. I've walked it. I've talked it. I've fought the battles. And I am sharing what I've learned with you. Are you ready to learn some of the enemy's tactics?

Deuteronomy 28 was written thousands of years ago; its concepts and principles were not discovered yesterday. Everyone likes to read the first half of the chapter, which explains all the positive and wonderful blessings that occur when you walk in obedience to God. However, most people don't continue on with the curses of disobedience listed in the second half of that chapter.

You must understand that there are both blessings *and* curses. We, you and I, make the choice to walk in either blessings or curses. In this context, the term *curse* does not mean taking God's name in vain, swearing, or using an obscenity that is unacceptable in most cultured environments. It simply means the opposite of a blessing. Blessings include all the good, positive things that happen to you and around you. Curses include all the bad, negative things.

> **We, you and I, make the choice to walk in either blessings or curses.**

Power of Your Words

We all desperately want to enjoy God's blessings. Everyone loves blessings—fun, joy, love, finances, good friends, a great life. However, life is not all fun and games. Everything has its place. Everything has two sides: positive and negative.

For instance, electricity runs all of our gadgets and allows us to illuminate our homes; however, if you stick your finger in an electrical outlet, you will discover the negative, painful effects of electrical current. Balance is the key. To make an intelligent choice about your spiritual life, you have to know about the latter part of Deuteronomy—the other side of the coin.

How do we mess up? Do we block our blessings? Did our ancestors do something to hinder God's will for our lives? Has someone spoken curses over us to separate us from His perfect will?

God is positive. Believers know Satan is negative. The two are total opposites. Both are fighting for our commitment, our devotion, our obedience, our choice. Blessings come from God. Curses come from Satan. If we follow God's principles, we bless others, as well as draw blessings upon ourselves. If we follow Satan's influence, we will speak curses upon others and draw the same upon ourselves.

Have you cursed anyone? I don't mean swearing at someone. Cursing someone can be as simple as saying something negative to him or about him. Have you ever said something that did not edify, exhort, correct in love, or confirm another person? Of course, we all have.

Have you ever brought something into your home that had negative spiritual effects on your environment? Children are especially vulnerable and innocent about falling for the offbeat, the weird, the strange, and the unwittingly demonic things of the world. *Dungeons and Dragons*, Ouija boards, Halloween, off-color music, the Harry Potter movies and books, and creatures of darkness can be portrayed as "fun." Movies and books quietly introduce and encourage "the powers of darkness" as innocent fun.

The Bible explains that Satan can be disguised as *"an angel of light"* (2 Corinthians 11:14). Many false religions portray their tools as beautiful things, masking what they truly are—objects of darkness. Beautiful statues, clothes, and people appear to be godly representations, while instead they are only illusions to draw the innocent away from God. If the believer isn't aware of both sides of the "coin," he or she can—and probably will—get caught in Satan's trap. Even worse, if other members of the family aren't prepared to fight the fight of faith, they can be drawn into darkness, as well. Satan is very subtle. He speaks quiet suggestions and makes things look *so* good as he draws people into his trap.

You Become What You Seek

We tend to take on the identities of those things around us—words, environments, or other people. For instance, we are strongly influenced by our parents when we are young. Often, children want to be "just like mom or dad" when they grow up. Teenagers encourage their peers to belong and "fit in" to be popular and accepted. We tend to talk the same, dress the same, and act the same as our friends.

If you hear positive affirmations, you are usually built up to meet those expectations. If negative vibes are shot in your direction, you can also meet those expectations. Your personality plays a big part. If you are a people pleaser, you will conform more readily to the suggestions of others. Strong and aggressive people will experiment with the offbeat and unusual aspects of life, often dragging others along their crooked paths.

The enemy sneaks around in any way possible; sometimes he is obvious, but usually he operates in very subtle ways that are almost impossible to recognize. Apparently innocent words, common sayings, or cute objects can have negative spiritual connotations that are hidden from the uninformed.

Don't be ignorant or unaware. (See 2 Corinthians 2:11.) Listen and learn. Protect your life, your family, and your friends. Ask God for open ears, open eyes, and an open heart to learn, understand, and discern God's truth from the enemy's lies and deceptions. Empower yourself and those you love with the weapons to fight.

We must accept responsibility for our actions and words. We open the door and welcome the blessings. In reality, we are also responsible for allowing the curses, the negative, into our lives. In reverse, we can also *prevent* or block both the blessings and the curses from entering our lives.

No one is exempt from God's commandments, rules, or precepts. The Bible is full of examples and wisdom to follow as we endeavor to reach what God has planned for us. We will never have all the answers. We will not reach the ultimate rung of the ladder. Only Jesus did that. We will search all our lives for answers, but our souls will not be totally perfected until we reach heaven.

In the meantime, we are going to examine areas in which we might have opened doors for the enemy to enter. We will learn how to get him out and keep him out of our lives. Where do we find God's answer to this situation? The wisdom, the knowledge for living successfully, is found within the pages of the Bible, God's Word.

The Bible Is Our Ultimate Guide

Just as we live and develop differently, we talk differently, react differently, and understand things differently. God knows this, and He has written His Word in ways to fit all our needs and interests. Amazingly, the Bible is written in ways that will appeal to all of us.

For example, if you enjoy interesting historical facts, you will read the Bible to discover how people lived, thought, and worked in ancient times. It is a fascinating historical account of unique people—our ancestors. We can learn how they handled all aspects of life: physical, mental, social, financial, and spiritual. We can learn from their mistakes and be inspired by their triumphs.

If you want to know how God blesses His children, you will search for His precious promises: His love, His blessings, eternal life, positive reinforcement, reassurance that He is in control, peace because He knows the answers, and faith that He is the Truth. Reading His promises truly calms the spirit. During a battle, put cards printed with these promises around your environment to remind yourself that God truly is in control. It is also a great way to memorize His Word.

Some people read the Bible out of habit. Perhaps they started reading it daily as young children or have been taught that reading the Bible every day is necessary for their salvation. Of course, feeding on God's Word regularly is very important. The Bible instructs us to meditate on it both day and night. (See Psalm 1:2.) However, if you do it only out of duty, you will be filled with guilt if you miss a day. I am a great proponent of reading the Bible as much as you can, but I don't feel guilty if I have to skip a day. When you read from duty, you probably won't receive any great revelations.

You can read the Bible and make it very personal. For instance, my Bible is written in a special way. It says, "For God so loved *Joan* that He gave His only begotten Son, that *if Joan* believes in Him *she will* not perish but have everlasting life." In many places throughout my Bible, I have scratched out the name that was originally printed there and replaced it with my name instead. Because my Bible was written just for me, it is God's love letter to *Joan Hunter.* Your Bible is His personal letter to you.

When you read the Bible from duty, you probably won't receive any great revelations.

There are times when you can open up the Bible and just say, "God, speak to me through Your Word," and He will speak to you as you study His Word. I don't advocate opening the Bible blindfolded, pointing to a random verse, and expecting an answer. I also won't say that you will never get your answer doing that, but usually, you need to read over a period of time before the answer suddenly appears or is revealed to you.

Prophesy the Word

God also revealed to me that we can read the Word prophetically. What does that mean? Read His promises. Believe His promises. Find one that is near and dear to your heart, read it, and meditate on it.

The Word of God says that we should want to prophesy. If you need a prophetic Word, prophesy over yourself! Read the verse out loud. Post those special verses on 3×5 cards in conspicuous places where you will see and read them often. Repeat them out loud every time you see them. See them, read them, hear them, and absorb the message, the blessing. Prophesy the Word to yourself.

If the Word of God is in you, if the power of God is in you, if the authority of Jesus Christ is in you, then you will get a word of knowledge, you will hear His voice, and you will know what you need to prophesy to yourself. Look at yourself in the mirror. Point to your reflection in the mirror and speak words in agreement with His Word to the face you see: "You are going to live. You are not going to die. I have called you without a shadow of a doubt. You are going to do great and mighty things for Me." Prophesy over yourself.

People come to me and say, "I need a word from you." No, you don't need a word from me; you need a word from God. I will tell you to get into the Bible, read His Word, and ask God to reveal His Word to you. That's the word I would give you before I would say anything else.

God has blessed me with the gift of prophecy. If the time arises and the need is there, I will prophesy when He gives me the direction to do so. I am not going to say, "God's got great things for you." The Word already tells you that, and as a believer, you should already know God's got great things for you. There is nothing supernatural or prophetic about that because I can easily say it without feeling His anointing.

Learn, absorb, and soak in the Word of God so that you can spread His living water all over your environment—at home, at church, at work, and in your neighborhood. The more you give out to others, the more you take in. God's living water, His anointing, will just flow through you. Personally, I don't want to be a reservoir for the anointing; I want to be a river. I want Him to work through me to touch everyone I come into contact with—whether in meetings, through my teaching CDs, or through my books. Don't you want Him to work through you, too?

Prophesying the Word over yourself brings His promises into the *now*! One of the most predominant Scriptures in this ministry is Ephesians 1:17–19. I can read this as history or as God's promise to me, but I can also read this as a prophecy—not only to me, but to you, as well. God can take this Scripture and illuminate it to your heart, making it more real now than ever before. I will prophesy its message directly to you. Read this aloud:

> The God of our Lord Jesus Christ, the Father of glory, is giving
> to you the spirit of wisdom and revelation in the knowledge of

Him (not only of Him, but in all areas of your life), that the eyes of your understanding are going to be opened and enlightened, that you may know what is the hope of His calling—what He has called you to do. You are going to experience the riches of the glory of the inheritance in the saints and what is the exceeding greatness of His power toward you because you believe according to the working of His mighty power.

But this day, He has given to you the spirit of wisdom and revelation in the knowledge of Him—not only in the knowledge of Him in a spiritual sense, but the knowledge of Him in every area of your life. If you need wisdom in the area of your marriage, your home, your business, or your ministry, He is going to give you greater wisdom and knowledge than you have ever experienced in your life before. Amen.

The Lord God is saying to you that He is going to give you a spirit of wisdom and revelation and knowledge of Him like you have never experienced before in your life. As the eyes of your understanding are enlightened, He is opening your eyes to see things in the spirit realm, as well as in the natural realm, that you have never seen before.

In addition, you are going to know God's calling on your life. He is going to reveal to you His individualized plan for your life, and you are going to see the reason for which you were born on this earth. You are going to receive greater wisdom and knowledge of Him—who He is, what He can do, and everything about Him. You will have the knowledge of Him in your head and the presence of Him in your heart, and you will experience Him like never before.

You will know and understand the exceeding greatness of His power toward you because you believe. Because you believe, you are going to see things happen on your behalf and through your hands. And God's mighty power is not just working through me; it is coming down to flow in and through your life.

Will you receive that prophecy? I receive it every time I read or hear it. I love reading the Word of God, but reading it prophetically has excited me beyond words.

Expect Revelation

The next step is to expect His revelation. Look for it. Recognize what He is doing in your life. Give Him all the praise and all the glory. And then, expect much, much more.

"Call to Me, and I will answer you, and show you great and mighty things, which you do not know" (Jeremiah 33:3). Prophetically, in today's terms, God is saying, "You asked Me, and I'm going to show you things that no one else has seen!"

A couple was happily married for nineteen and a half years. Early in their marriage, the husband began to have an overwhelming interest in death. He planned his funeral at the age of twenty-four because he was confident that he would not live past his forty-second birthday.

Several years later, these two were very active and traveling in ministry. Without warning, he suddenly developed some serious symptoms, and he was diagnosed as having a collapsed lung due to cancer. He was given three months to live.

For a while, he seemed to get better. The wife did everything she knew to do. She fasted, prayed, and continued to minister with a great anointing. When she returned home from one of her meetings, she found her husband having difficulty walking. Medical experts found seventeen tumors on his spine. From that point on, things spiraled downward.

The wife continued in ministry, but her heart was full of questions. Why? What could she have done differently? Did she not have enough faith? She knew that only the Lord could give her the answers. After caring for her husband through nearly two years of surgery, treatments, and lengthy hospitalizations, she was exhausted physically, emotionally, and spiritually.

While she was sitting under anointed teaching of the Word, God began to answer her questions. The Lord reminded her that her husband had said over and over again that he would die before his forty-second birthday. The Lord also gave her a revelation of Mark 11:23 about getting what you say. If you confess negative things, you will receive the negative. If you speak positive things, you will receive the positive. Matthew 12:34 says that *out of the abundance of the heart the mouth speaks.* You will get what you say!

Although he worked in the ministry, this man of God had never repented, denounced, or cut off those words. He died. His faithful wife is still in ministry, teaching these truths and revelations to help others around the world to get free.

> *For assuredly, I say to you, whoever says to this mountain, "Be removed and be cast into the sea," and does not doubt in his heart, but believes that those things he says will be done, he will have whatever he says.* (Mark 11:23)

> *Keep your heart with all diligence, for out of it spring the issues of life.* (Proverbs 4:23)

> *A good man out of the good treasure of his heart brings forth good; and an evil man out of the evil treasure of his heart brings forth evil. For out of the abundance of the heart his mouth speaks.* (Luke 6:45)

> *Death and life are in the power of the tongue* [mouth]. (Proverbs 18:21)

Watch what you say! Your words are powerful!

CHAPTER 6

Don't Curse Your Blessings

There is one who speaks like the piercings of a sword, but the tongue of the wise promotes health. (Proverbs 12:18)

The heart of the wise teaches his mouth, and adds learning to his lips. Pleasant words are like a honeycomb, sweetness to the soul and health to the bones. (Proverbs 16:23–24)

Let the words of my mouth and the meditation of my heart be acceptable in Your sight, O LORD, my strength and my Redeemer. (Psalm 19:14)

And my speech and my preaching were not with persuasive words of human wisdom, but in demonstration of the Spirit and of power, that your faith should not be in the wisdom of men but in the power of God. (1 Corinthians 2:4–5)

He will bring you a message through which you and all your household will be saved. (Acts 11:14 NIV)

If you abide in Me, and My words abide in you, you will ask what you desire, and it shall be done for you. By this My Father is glorified, that you bear much fruit; so you will be My disciples. (John 15:7–8)

A rough word can destroy like a sword stabbing through the heart, but a wise, uplifting comment can soothe the spirit and bring peace and a smile.

We have all heard the saying, "If you can't say something good about someone, don't say anything at all!" It is not a quotation from the Bible, but the principle behind it is very scriptural.

What Do Your Words Do?

We had a lady come to a service where we were teaching on word curses. Through a word of knowledge, I knew someone was experiencing intense abdominal pain. The lady came forward. I described what I felt in my spirit was wrong with her, and she confirmed my words. Before I could pray with her, she said, "Wait, I have to tell you something."

Because of her many abdominal problems, she had gone to the doctor for a diagnostic procedure. Her intestines were so twisted that the procedure could not be completed. She explained, "When I was a teenager, every time I saw my mom, I would say, 'I hate you so much you make my intestines twist and turn. Every time I see you, my intestines just twist.'"

Her intestines had obeyed her words. They had entangled themselves, causing her years of suffering and pain. I had her say a prayer of forgiveness over her father and mother and then asked her to repeat the following: "In Jesus' name, I renounce those words that I spoke about my mother and over my intestines."

At that point, I laid my hands on her abdominal area. I could feel movement all over the area. I said, "In the name of Jesus, I command these intestines to go back into their proper place. I command them to function normally. I command all pain to go." Suddenly, her abdomen was quiet and still. Her pain was gone.

> *Anyone who receives a prophet because he is a prophet will receive a prophet's reward, and anyone who receives a righteous man because he is a righteous man will receive a righteous man's reward.*
> (Matthew 10:41 NIV)

The Word says that if you honor a prophet, you will receive a prophet's reward. What does that mean? In one of the Bible's Old Testament stories, the Shunamite woman fed and took care of the prophet Elisha. In return, God blessed her with a son within the year. (See 2 Kings 4:8–17.) She received her reward.

> **A prophet is always symbolic—a type and shadow of God.**

A prophet is always symbolic—a type and shadow of God. Thus, the woman was serving God as she served the prophet. She made room in her home for the prophet Elisha. She took care of him. She did everything possible to minister to him. He finally turned to her and asked, "What do you want?"

God is asking you, "What do you want?" Think about it. What do you want? The Bible says, *"You don't have what you want because you don't ask God for it"* (James 4:2 NLT).

Many people have spoken prophetically over my life, including Kim Clement, Mark Chironna, Charles and Beryl Dixon, the Tolersons, and others. They have spoken some incredible, unbelievable prophetic words over me. Hearing them, I thought to myself, *Oh, that's impossible. Not me.* Then, I realized that the incredible words came directly from God. "Oh, yes, I accept every word, God! Thank You! Thank You! Thank You!"

Most of these prophecies are so amazing that there's absolutely no way I can ever accomplish them without God. Of course, that is the way He likes it. He usually asks us to do the impossible, such as heal somebody, knowing we can't do it without Him. And because you can't do it alone, you have to know and acknowledge that it is Him working through you.

When I get up in the morning, I say, "Father, I bless Mark Chironna, I bless Kim Clement, I bless the Tolersons, I bless the Dixons, I bless all the people who have blessed me. I bless all those who have spoken good things over me. I bless Your prophets. I bless those friends You have brought into my life. I bless all those men and women of God who have affected my life. I bless them all in the name of Jesus."

And do you know why? I want to receive what they have spoken over me.

I will raise up for them a Prophet like you from among their brethren, and will put My words in His mouth, and He shall speak to them all that I command Him. And it shall be that whoever will not hear My

words, which He speaks in My name, I will require it of him.
(Deuteronomy 18:18–19)

When you bless the people who have prophesied over you, you will be blessed. For example, say your pastor preached a great message. It was an exciting service. Later, when you had lunch on Sunday afternoon, you talked about the pastor and his wife in a negative manner. If you did that, do not expect to be blessed.

If the pastor of your church speaks prosperity and blessing over you and later you go home and criticize his tie, his haircut, or some other aspect of his life, then you cut off the blessings that he just spoke over you. You are cursing your blessings. You are opening the door to problems.

Now, I'm talking to you, preaching to you, and prophesying to you that the eyes of your understanding are going to be enlightened and that you're going to flow in greater wisdom and knowledge than you have ever experienced in your life.

It is your choice what you do from here. Will you criticize and cut off your blessing, or will you pray for me and bless me because I want you to walk in all the blessings and healing that God has to offer? *"Not that I seek the gift, but I seek the fruit that abounds to your account"* (Philippians 4:17).

God directs all blessings into my life. My desire is for you to be blessed. Bless your pastors, bless those who have authority over you, bless your boss, and open your arms to receive the blessings from your Father.

> *"Death and life are in the power of the tongue."*
> **I choose life.**

What I am teaching you can transform your life. You are going to see greater freedom and breakthroughs in every area of your life. *"I have set before you life and death, blessing and cursing; therefore choose life, that both you and your descendants may live"* (Deuteronomy 30:19). *"Death and life are in the power of the tongue"* (Proverbs 18:21). I choose life.

"You have as little to fear from an undeserved curse

as from the dart of a wren or the swoop of a swallow" (Proverbs 26:2 MSG). A curse cannot stick without a cause. If you're having financial trouble, ask yourself what door you have opened up to allow that curse of poverty to enter your life. God likes firstfruits. Give Him the firstfruits of your harvest, and He will bless you with more than enough.

If you have been saying negative words about another person, remember that negative words about you may have their effects. If you keep your silence, then any negative words (curses) sent in your direction will fall short of your door. They will be blocked from having an effect on your life. The choice is ultimately yours. What you give is what you get.

> *Give, and it will be given to you: good measure, pressed down, shaken together, and running over will be put into your bosom. For with the same measure that you use, it will be measured back to you.*
>
> (Luke 6:38)

Everybody loves that Scripture. We read it, memorize it, claim it, and stand on it. However, there are three other verses that we need to consider before we get to verse 38.

> *Love your enemies, do good, and lend, hoping for nothing in return; and your reward will be great, and you will be sons of the Most High. For He is kind to the unthankful and evil. Therefore be merciful, just as your Father also is merciful. Judge not, and you shall not be judged. Condemn not, and you shall not be condemned. Forgive, and you will be forgiven.* (Luke 6:35–37)

Try reading this passage from *The Message* Bible. You may find a whole new insight with this version.

> *To you who are ready for the truth, I say this: Love your enemies. Let them bring out the best in you, not the worst. When someone gives you a hard time, respond with the energies of prayer for that person. If someone slaps you in the face, stand there and take it. If someone grabs your shirt, giftwrap your best coat and make a present of it. If*

someone takes unfair advantage of you, use the occasion to practice the servant life. No more tit-for-tat stuff. Live generously.

Here is a simple rule of thumb for behavior: Ask yourself what you want people to do for you; then grab the initiative and do it for them! If you only love the lovable, do you expect a pat on the back? Run-of-the-mill sinners do that. If you only help those who help you, do you expect a medal? Garden-variety sinners do that. If you only give for what you hope to get out of it, do you think that's charity? The stingiest of pawnbrokers does that.

I tell you, love your enemies. Help and give without expecting a return. You'll never—I promise—regret it. Live out this God-created identity the way our Father lives toward us, generously and graciously, even when we're at our worst. Our Father is kind; you be kind.

Don't pick on people, jump on their failures, criticize their faults—unless, of course, you want the same treatment. Don't condemn those who are down; that hardness can boomerang. Be easy on people; you'll find life a lot easier. Give away your life; you'll find life given back, but not merely given back—given back with bonus and blessing. Giving, not getting, is the way. Generosity begets generosity.

(Luke 6:27–38 MSG)

Many are familiar with the blessings and curses of Deuteronomy 28. There is an abundance of blessings in obedience, and there is an equal abundance of curses associated with disobedience. This applies to many areas of life. God might tell you to speak to someone or say something, and then you don't do it. You disobey. God might tell you to pray for somebody, and you don't obey. Disobedience is sin. Thank God that you can repent and pray for the next one He brings to you for ministry.

My desire is for you to be blessed. You need to be out of debt, you need to be healed and whole, and you need to be free and prepared to do whatever God asks you to do and to go wherever He asks you to go.

What Is the Prophetic?

> **There are no time limits in the prophetic. Whenever you hear a prophetic word, it is for anybody who claims it as his own.**

There are no time limits in the prophetic. Whenever you hear a prophetic word, it is for anybody who wants it, reads it, and claims it as his own. In return, pray and bless the prophet who spoke it.

A certain prophet going around the nation has an incredible ministry. He doesn't wear a suit and tie, and he doesn't do his hair the way the average person does. His music is louder than some may like. He doesn't fit the mental image most people have of a prophet. If you recall, neither did the prophets of the Old Testament. However, none of today's prophets has been coughed out of a whale (see Jonah 1:17, 2:10) or has had to lie on his side for over a year (see Ezekiel 4:4–9).

People have often criticized this prophet. Instead of accepting the prophetic words of blessing he has spoken over them, many people have chosen to reject the blessing with critical words of derision. As soon as these people spoke negative words, their blessings were cut off.

This prophet has spoken great words over me. I bless him in the name of Jesus. He can wear his hair any way he wants to wear his hair. He can play music as loud as he wants to play music. He has a heart after God, and so I receive the word that he has prophesied over the body of Christ. I receive that word personally, in Jesus' name.

I also receive it for the ministry in the name of Jesus, as well as for each one reading this book. Prophecy doesn't end when the words have been spoken. Written words can be read year after year with the same effect. The Bible's promises don't end the first time you read them. Prophecy lasts.

"Do not touch My anointed ones, and do My prophets no harm" (1

Chronicles 16:22). Do not touch God's anointed. Only God understands what kind of person or what kind of words will reach another person. One pastor or Christian leader might not "speak" to you. You might not understand why a certain Christian teacher seems to be able to "read your mail."

Everyone responds differently to a certain message. You might get inspired by a particular speaker while your friend or spouse doesn't like that person at all. Your lost son or daughter might get saved through the ministry someone with strange clothes, piercings, or tattoos. Only God knows what will work for any particular person. There is not just one way to reach everyone.

We are all at different levels of spiritual growth. Our vocabularies and our methods of learning are unique. Just because someone doesn't totally minister to you or totally agree with your opinions or beliefs doesn't mean that the person isn't chosen or anointed by God. Pray wisdom over the speaker. Pray a blessing over that person and ask God to take care of him or her, giving correction if needed. Keep your tongue silent about the problems with other Christians.

Just as God makes every snowflake different, He creates each person with unique traits. Recognize the fact that there are differences in ministry and differences among His ministers. Don't criticize your pastor. Don't criticize me. Don't criticize people on Christian television. Just bless them in the name of Jesus.

If you feel like they're preaching something wrong, pray for God to reveal it to them. Ask Him to send His Holy Spirit to speak to them. You don't need to be the Holy Spirit, and you don't need to be criticizing. You have a choice regarding what you listen to and watch.

A good example of this is the difference in ministry fifty years ago compared with what is happening today. People change. Some people love the King James Version of the Bible. Others get lost with King James' English and choose the *New International Version* or *The Living Bible*

> **Obedience to God is the important factor, not conforming to what man or denominations claim to be necessary.**

instead. What attracts people seventy years old won't necessarily attract people who are twenty.

This applies to the delivery of the Word all the way down to the music people listen to and the clothing they wear. Each of us appeals to a different group of people because God has called us to minister to different people in different areas. You cannot judge what others need to hear or how they need to receive ministry. Obedience to God is the important factor, not conforming to what man or denominations claim to be necessary to fulfill God's call on our lives.

Death and Life Are in Your Words

Death and life are in the power of the tongue, and those who love it will eat its fruit.   (Proverbs 18:21)

You have heard that verse from Proverbs before, and you will hear it again. It is a powerful statement. We have all fallen short. We all are sinners, and we will have to repent many times each day for the rest of our lives. God has made a way for us—through repentance—to reconcile ourselves back to Him. It is my choice; it is your choice. Are you speaking death to yourself and your family? Or are you speaking life? Every word is a seed planted. What kind of fruit will your seeds (your words) yield? What kind of fruit will you have to eat?

A pastor friend called me to explain that something was not right in his church. He did not know what was retarding church growth. He was preaching the Word, people were getting healed, people were getting saved, and then those people were going elsewhere to attend church. He and his wife had prayed, and then they called me for advice.

When he was very young, this pastor had done some things that were not very nice. I do not know what he did, and I don't want to know what he did—I don't need the specifics. After becoming a pastor, he confessed what he had done to a visiting evangelist. The evangelist's response was, "Your church is never going to grow because of what you did in your past." Those negative words were a curse on that church. Growth stopped from that day forward until the day I prayed and broke that curse. Since I prayed, the church has grown consistently.

Some of you are dealing with health situations. You saw the physician, who explained that you have a terminal disease. What do you do next? Get worried, cry, get hysterical, or panic? No. Cut those words off, in Jesus' name. Don't get worried about your health; just give the situation to the Lord. Pray specifically for your symptoms or disease, give God all the glory, and then move on. Pray like this:

> Father, I release my health to You, in Jesus' name. I claim Your promises over my life. I have work to do for You, Father. I do not receive words of death and destruction from the doctor. I receive Your words of life and prosperity. Thank You, Father, in Jesus' name. Amen.

For years, I thought I couldn't minister to others because of my past. Perhaps you are experiencing similar thoughts. Whether you are telling yourself that you are unqualified or whether other people are speaking those negative words to you, know right here, right now, today, that everyone can be and will be used of God. The only qualifying factor is being willing to be used.

You are not on trial for your past mistakes. If the blood of Jesus Christ washes away all sin, it washes away *all* sin—period. What you did in the past does not make any difference. That's why it is called *the past*. It can affect your future only if you let it—*only* if you let it.

You have minds like a snake pit! How do you suppose what you say is worth anything when you are so foul-minded? It's your heart, not the dictionary, that gives meaning to your words. A good person produces good deeds and words season after season. An evil person is a blight on the orchard. Let me tell you something: Every one of these

69

careless words is going to come back to haunt you. There will be a time of Reckoning. Words are powerful; take them seriously. Words can be your salvation. Words can also be your damnation.
(Matthew 12:35–37 MSG)

How many of you have said words that did not edify, exhort, correct in love, or confirm? Those words are called careless (or idle) words. We have all said words that did not edify, exhort, correct in love, or confirm. People have said those careless words over you, also. When I hear those words today, I just cut them off in the name of Jesus.

A variety of negative "curses" were spoken over me in my early years. I lived "down" to what they said about me. When I realized that those words were not what God's Word said about me, my entire life changed. But first, I had to break the word curses that had been spoken over me. You are the only one who can break the word curses over you, because you are the one over whom they were spoken. If you want to pray for someone else, make sure that person is there to pray in agreement with you and break the curse that was spoken over his or her life.

Quite often, we respond out of habit. You may have to repent and cut off your habitual words many times before you get your tongue under control. What do I mean by that? The next story is a good example.

A friend of mine always got irritated with other drivers who cut her off in traffic. One day, she was about to yell at the driver who had just cut in front of her on a busy freeway when she noticed his bumper sticker: "God Loves You." She quickly bit her tongue and started laughing instead, "Thank You, Father! I got the message!"

The next time something like that happens to you, bless the driver in the name of Jesus and wave, "God bless you." Try it for yourself. You may find yourself pleasantly surprised when fewer people cut you off in traffic!

You need to break the word curses spoken over you and be free of them. First, you need to repent of the negative words you have spoken over other people; then, in turn, you can walk out from under the curses that have been spoken over you. Once again, no curse can stick without a cause. (See Proverbs 26:2.) If you have cursed somebody (spoken negative words over somebody else), you need to repent. Eventually, you will learn to control your tongue, because from this day forward, you're going to have a greater level of accountability about your words than you have ever had before.

No curse can stick without a cause.

> Father, I have said words that did not edify, exhort, correct in love, or confirm. I repent of those words, and I renounce them in Jesus' name. I ask You to bless anyone whom I have spoken ill words over. And likewise, based on my repentance, any words that have been spoken over me that did not edify, exhort, correct in love, or confirm are now broken off of me, in Jesus' name. Amen.

Once I broke those curses, anything negative spoken over me was broken. Any negative confession over my finances was broken off of me. Any words spoken against me, especially regarding my health, were broken off of me. The words that said I would never amount to anything or be anything were broken off of me, in Jesus' name. Hallelujah!

If you prayed the above prayer, you should feel much better. Most people claim to feel lighter and taller when they stand up. The burdens they were carrying are gone.

> *If your enemy is hungry, give him bread to eat; and if he is thirsty, give him water to drink; for so you will heap coals of fire on his head, and the LORD will reward you.* (Proverbs 25:21–22)

Bless those who curse you. Since the Word says to bless your enemies, start off speaking good things about them. Speak positive words of blessing over them, and those blessings will return to you. Watching things turn around will be exciting. Don't hesitate to give God all the praise when you see what He does.

Father, in the name of Jesus, I give You the glory. I thank You for what You have done, and I thank You for the word curses that have been broken off of me. Father, I thank You for greater freedom than I have ever experienced before in my life. Father, I thank You that You are going to show me if I say anything from this day forward that does not edify, exhort, correct in love, or confirm. And in the event that I do, I will repent immediately, in Jesus' name. Father, I thank You for Your grace, and I thank You for Your forgiveness, in Jesus' name. Amen.

CHAPTER 7

What's in Your House?

The children of Israel committed a trespass regarding the accursed things, for Achan the son of Carmi, the son of Zabdi, the son of Zerah, of the tribe of Judah, took of the accursed things; so the anger of the LORD burned against the children of Israel. (Joshua 7:1)

Do you know someone who appears to live a perfect life? He doesn't seem to have any issues or problems to deal with. She always seems to have the right words at the right time. Suddenly, this person is weeping at the altar one day, and no one can figure out what could possibly be wrong with this "perfect" individual.

No one is perfect—and no one can know the hidden secrets and sins of the heart. These are the battles we fight every day. Outwardly, everything appears to be perfect, a good life; but inwardly, you might harbor all types of hidden problems. No one wants to admit to having impure thoughts or hidden sins. These heart issues have powerful effects on our lives, whether hidden or not. Other people's problems can also affect our lives.

Whenever you get sick, examine yourself first. Ask yourself, *Is there any way, any avenue, in which I've opened myself to some sin—a sin of disobedience, a sin of not giving—any sin, blatant or hidden? Is there anything in my life blocking my relationship with God and His protection?*

Years ago, I prayed for a family in whose household all hell had broken loose. The daughter had broken her leg, the wife had undergone surgery, and the husband had been hit in the mouth with such force that his jaw was broken. He couldn't work, and he lost more than half of his income. Every single one of their family members got sick. It had been going on for about three months when I pulled the father aside, away from his family, and asked, "What has been going on in your life the last four months?"

He admitted, "Well, I did a certain thing. I know that it is wrong. I just can't give it up." As the head of the house, this man had opened the door to sin. We prayed, and he repented; then, all heaven broke loose in their home!

This man was the head of the house, and he had lost his spiritual control and protection over the home. His actions had a specific effect on his home and family. Once he resumed his position as spiritual head of his home and family, protection and blessings returned.

> **If you are in a battle, the first thing to do is examine yourself.**

If you are in a battle, the first thing to do is examine yourself. Many times, we believe that we didn't say or do anything wrong. We claim, "It wasn't me!" Unfortunately, quite often, we are the cause of our own problems. Pride comes in and blinds us as we claim, "I'm too perfect to have caused this problem." Pride alone can open that door. Always examine yourself for open doors where sickness may have gained entrance. Any sin can give the enemy permission to come into your life when you have walked away from the blessings of God.

Communion

In the same manner He also took the cup after supper, saying, "This cup is the new covenant in My blood. This do, as often as you drink it, in remembrance of Me." For as often as you eat this bread and drink this cup, you proclaim the Lord's death till He comes.

Therefore whoever eats this bread or drinks this cup of the Lord in an unworthy manner will be guilty of the body and blood of the Lord. But let a man examine himself, and so let him eat of the bread and drink of the cup. For he who eats and drinks in an unworthy manner eats and drinks judgment to himself, not discerning the Lord's body.

For this reason many are weak and sick among you, and many sleep. (1 Corinthians 11:25–30)

According to God's Word, if we do not take Communion correctly, we can become sick. Can we do—or fail to do—other things that can cause illness or disease? Yes, we can. We all have a responsibility to know how to live within God's perfect will. To live in today's world, we have rules to live by and laws to follow. In the spiritual world, we also have directions to follow.

The Word of God says that if you take His bread, you can be made whole. There is healing during participation in Communion. Before we take Communion, God asks us to repent of our sins and not to take Communion without forgiving others.

This is the bread which comes down from heaven, that one may eat of it and not die. I am the living bread which came down from heaven. If anyone eats of this bread, he will live forever; and the bread that I shall give is My flesh, which I shall give for the life of the world. (John 6:50–51)

Blood Covenants

There are three covenants that God considers holy. When someone made a covenant with God in the Old Testament, the men were circumcised. *"You shall be circumcised in the flesh of your foreskins, and it shall be a sign of the covenant between Me and you"* (Genesis 17:11). Circumcision identified a man as a follower of God.

In the New Testament age, circumcision is no longer required, as the sign of the covenant is immersion baptism. Being baptized in water is an outward indication of your covenant with God. Non-Christian religions may tolerate Christian converts until water baptism occurs. Then, the new Christian is ostracized and kicked out of his previous religion. If you haven't been baptized by immersion since being saved, I strongly advise you to do so. The covenant is so important.

Marriage with intercourse is a holy covenant between two people.

When a man and a woman come together after marriage in the act of intimacy, they are making a holy covenant with each other. There is a shedding of blood when the hymen is broken. Any sexual relations outside of marriage are considered an unholy or ungodly covenant.

If you haven't renounced unholy covenants that you made before marriage, you are still connected by covenant to the other people. As with blood covenants, everything you have is theirs and everything they have is yours. This does not mean only ownership of the house, car, other possessions, or children. There is a serious spiritual component.

They are no longer two but one flesh. Therefore what God has joined together, let not man separate. (Matthew 19:6)

For out of the heart proceed evil thoughts, murders, adulteries, fornications, thefts, false witness, blasphemies. These are the things which defile a man, but to eat with unwashed hands does not defile a man. (Matthew 15:19–20)

You say, "Food was made for the stomach, and the stomach for food." (This is true, though someday God will do away with both of them.) But you can't say that our bodies were made for sexual immorality. They were made for the Lord, and the Lord cares about our bodies. And God will raise us from the dead by his power, just as he raised our Lord from the dead. Don't you realize that your bodies are actually parts of Christ? Should a man take his body, which is part of Christ, and join it to a prostitute? Never! And don't you realize that if a man joins himself to a prostitute, he becomes one body with her? For the Scriptures say, "The two are united into one." But the person who is joined to the Lord is one spirit with him. (1 Corinthians 6:13–17 NLT)

Flee sexual immorality. Every sin that a man does is outside the body, but he who commits sexual immorality sins against his own body. Or do you not know that your body is the temple of the Holy

Spirit who is in you, whom you have from God, and you are not your own? For you were bought at a price; therefore glorify God in your body and in your spirit, which are God's. (1 Corinthians 6:18–20)

In Him you were also circumcised with the circumcision made without hands, by putting off the body of the sins of the flesh, by the circumcision of Christ, buried with Him in baptism, in which you also were raised with Him through faith in the working of God, who raised Him from the dead. And you, being dead in your trespasses and the uncircumcision of your flesh, He has made alive together with Him, having forgiven you all trespasses, having wiped out the handwriting of requirements that was against us, which was contrary to us. And He has taken it out of the way, having nailed it to the cross.

(Colossians 2:11–14)

God made a blood covenant with Abraham in the Old Testament. David and Jonathan made a blood covenant with each other. We don't practice the actual shedding or mingling of blood between people in covenants these days. However, the breaking of the woman's hymen is the sign of the covenant between a husband and wife.

When my ex-husband was out in the bars doing ungodly things, I was still in covenant with him. I didn't want to be joined to all that sin. Even after we were divorced, I still had to break and renounce the covenant we had made many years before. I didn't have to break the emotional "soul ties," however, as I had broken those much earlier.

"Marriage is honorable among all, and the bed undefiled; but fornicators and adulterers God will judge" (Hebrews 13:4). Have you ever felt strange, later to find out that your ex-spouse was doing ungodly things? You are still in covenant with that person and his or her actions. Renounce that covenant. Break it.

Recently, a friend of mine was preparing to get married, and she came to me for information on breaking previous covenants. She knew the importance of breaking all the covenants she had developed prior

Renounce all ungodly covenants.

to her marriage, and she wanted to make sure that everything was covered. She wanted a whole heart and a pure relationship with her husband-to-be.

Renounce all ungodly covenants. If you were married before and your spouse died, I believe that death has broken the covenant. However, I always encourage people to renounce the covenant anyway.

If you have been married before and have had sexual relations within the boundaries of marriage but are no longer married, repeat this prayer:

Father, I went into covenant with _____. I am no longer married to _____. In Jesus' name, I renounce that covenant. Anything bad that came into my life because of that relationship, take it from me now, in Jesus' name. Thank You, Jesus.

Many people, both inside and outside the Christian community, believe that it is normal to have sex with people other than their spouses. Spouses may not be accessible, so some believe they need to seek satisfaction and comfort from anyone willing and available. This behavior is not acceptable. It is compromise. It is sin.

Many churches don't correct—or feel like they can't correct—aberrant behavior within their leadership or congregations. This ungodly behavior affects not only the life and relationships of the person in question, but it also compromises the entire church and its ministry to others.

If you have had any relations outside of marriage, pray this prayer:

Father, I entered into an ungodly covenant with _____. This was sin. Take this sin from me, never to be remembered or held against me again. This covenant I made with _____ is now broken, in Jesus' name. Thank You, Jesus. Amen.

Now, repeat that prayer for each person with whom you made an ungodly covenant. Doing this will not only set you free, it will allow you to minister the same freedom to others.

Keeping mercy for thousands, forgiving iniquity and transgression and sin, by no means clearing the guilty, visiting the iniquity of the fathers upon the children and the children's children to the third and the fourth generation. (Exodus 34:7)

Children born from an ungodly covenant can be affected by generational curses to the third or fourth generation. Cover your ancestors' sins and break ungodly covenants as far back as necessary.

Sin gives the enemy permission to come in and cause problems. When you sin, you open up the door for sickness, illness, curses, and disasters. Repentance opens up the door for healing and restoration, whether it be physical, mental, or financial. Look for any doors you may have opened. Self-examination comes first. Then, look for generational curses as a possible root.

> **Repentance opens up the door for healing and restoration, whether it be physical, mental, or financial.**

Unforgiveness, anger, bitterness, resentment, fear, stress, sexual sins, rebellion, and generational curses are just some of the things that can open the door. Another "door opener" can be word curses, which we discussed in the previous two chapters. We must start with our own problems, our own heart issues, and get rid of those things so we can live fruitful lives.

Generational Curses

You shall not make for yourself a carved image; any likeness of anything that is in heaven above, or that is in the earth beneath, or that is in the water under the earth; you shall not bow down to them nor serve them. For I, the LORD your God, am a jealous God, visiting the iniquity of the fathers upon the children to the third and fourth generations of those who hate Me, but showing mercy to thousands, to those who love Me and keep My commandments.

(Deuteronomy 5:8–10)

Sin can open the door for sickness. However, it does not have to be your sin. It can also be generational sins from your ancestors. Occasionally, you can track specific effects through the generations. A few examples would be the repeated occurrence of mental problems, heart problems, divorce, anger, or abuse through numerous family members. These curses can be broken. If your family history is sketchy or incomplete, praying to break the generational curses that you suspect are present is not a bad idea. The prayer may have a powerful, positive effect on the person you are praying for, bringing total healing into his or her life.

Since generational curses are brought down through the bloodline, is there anything we should know about blood transfusions and transplants?

A lady who had received blood transfusions came to one of my schools with ten things wrong with her health. When we went through the breaking of generational curses passed on through blood transfusions, she described feeling like a ton of pressure had been lifted off of her. Eight of those diseases left her *instantly*.

There were two people who received body part transplants from one cadaver. After the transplants, these people would fall asleep and feel like they were falling. To make a long story short, the donated organs had come from a person who had died in a falling accident.

A pastor's wife received a blood transfusion. When the infusion was complete, she called her husband to tell him that she felt like she had received blood from a "party animal" because she just wanted to go out and party! She felt *completely* different after the prayer.

After another sweet young lady received a heart transplant, she started having nightmares about being stabbed to death. After several days of this, she called in a police artist to make a composite sketch of the person in her nightmares. They discovered that her transplanted heart had come from a woman who had been stabbed to death. Based on the sketch and other confirming evidence, the murderer was arrested. After prayer, she had no more nightmares.

Would I refuse a blood transfusion if I needed one? Let me emphasize this right now: if I need blood, give me a blood transfusion. I know what to do. My husband knows what to do. Prayer will cut off any negative effects connected to the donor.

At one point, I had to have some cadaver bone tissue put in a "hole" in my skull. Along with a friend, I prayed the prayer I'm about to share with you, and we both saw something like fumes leave my body. I know this is real, because it happened to me.

> **Prayer should be utilized before, during, and after every treatment for any physical problem you might face.**

From my experience, I know that prayer never hurts anything. If a prayer relieves a problem, I believe the revelation is truly from God. Prayer should be utilized before, during, and after every treatment for any physical problem you might face.

> Father, I repent of sin on behalf of those whose blood I received. Take the sin from them and put it on the cross. In Jesus' name, I cut off any generational curse that may have entered in through this blood. Father, bless the person who donated this blood [or bless the family of the person who donated this body part, such as a heart, kidney, etc.] so I may live. Thank You, Father.

Should a Christian donate blood? *Yes!* First, evidence suggests that it is healthy for you to donate your blood. Second, you have the opportunity to bless your blood for others. Lay hands on the arm where the blood will be removed, and ask God to anoint it, draw people to Himself, and heal them through the life-giving blood. This is a type of prayer cloth that cannot be lost or misplaced. It is pure, clean, generational curse-free blood.

81

Obey God. Listen for His voice. He always has the best answers, and He knows the best way for you to be healed and whole.

Anger

Anger can enter your life because of unmet expectations. People do not meet your expectations; they don't do what you expect them to do. Anger walks in. The easiest way to illustrate this is to discuss the relationship between a husband and a wife. When a couple is married, the wife wakes up the first morning to discover that Prince Charming is really a frog—not literally, of course, but the man who was Mr. Perfect before the wedding is no longer perfect the next morning, or the next week.

After being married for two weeks, he still hasn't taken out the trash. He is not meeting his bride's expectations, and anger makes its entrance. Expectations and traditions should not be so important that they usher anger and sin into the relationship.

Many types of expectations between two people can go unmet. For example, your boss might have promised you something but didn't follow through; he didn't meet your expectations. He might have explained that you interpreted the information incorrectly, but you are angry because he did not deliver what he had promised.

It is very important that you deal with anger. Do not allow it to fester. Is anger a sin? The answer to that question is *no*—not initially, at least. However, uncontrolled anger can develop into sin and become very destructive. The Word says, *"Be angry, and do not sin"* (Psalm 4:4). It does not say, "If you are angry, you are in sin." Even Jesus got angry when He found money changers in the temple—an example of unmet expectations. (See John 2:14–17.)

If people claim to believe the Word of God and yet are doing things that are not of God, you can feel godly anger. You will then do whatever you can do in the spirit realm and in the natural realm to come against the ungodly actions. That type of anger is acceptable.

When unmet expectations are experienced day after day, the trash builds up into a mountain; other things start to pop up that are not handled in the way you want them to be done. The toothpaste cap is left off or the TV is turned up too loudly. Soon, the person in question can't meet *any* of your expectations. Anger builds up to a point where it becomes sin. It explodes in your heart and pours out into your life. Suddenly, you would be happier taking out your own trash and being single.

As silly as this example sounds, taking out the trash can become that important to some people. The problem is not the trash but what you do with the trash. One of Joyce Meyer's sayings is, "Pick your battles." Is the trash really worth arguing about? No! Just take it out yourself.

Don't be blind to your own problems. If your spouse isn't meeting your expectations, you are probably not meeting your spouse's expectations, either. You are not the perfect person about whom he or she was dreaming before the wedding. Reality takes hold, and you have to be the best you can be. Your spouse will have to accept you as you are and attempt to be the best that he or she can be. You will probably never meet all of your spouse's expectations. Instead, we all must work toward meeting God's expectations for us, not those of another person.

> **Don't be blind to your own problems.**

If you are harboring anger toward your spouse, children, or other family members, based on your unmet expectations for them, pray this prayer with me:

Father, I lay down my unmet expectations. I give them to You. I thank You for my children. I have had unrealistic expectations of my children. Father, I lay my unrealistic expectations for my spouse on Your altar. Also, I lay my unmet expectations for my parents on Your altar. Father, more importantly, I lay my unrealistic expectations for myself on Your altar. Nobody, including myself, will ever be able to live up to the high expectations that I have set. I release all my expectations to You. I lay them on Your altar. Father, I want to meet only Your expectations. Thank You for showing me how to do that, in Jesus' name. Amen.

What is in your heart? We are so quick to blame others. It is so easy to blame somebody else. Examine yourself, get rid of your pride, and make yourself a clean vessel to be used by God. Cut off any possible generational curses. Obey and listen only to Him.

Bitterness

Looking carefully lest anyone fall short of the grace of God; lest any root of bitterness springing up cause trouble, and by this many become defiled. (Hebrews 12:15)

Everybody has the opportunity to walk in anger, which can turn to bitterness. I choose to let those situations just roll off of me. Is it easy? *No.* But I have made my choice and will continue to do so. One night, my husband told me that I amazed him because I handle some very difficult situations and still go on doing what God has called me to do without allowing things to upset me.

Make the choice to deal with problems and then move on. Don't allow problems to fester, grow, and build until they explode into sin. Don't allow the roots of bitterness to squeeze the life out of your existence. Just give all the problems to God and allow Him to handle the situation.

If you are dealing with bitterness in your life, pray the following prayer with me:

Father, I lay my bitterness on Your altar. I don't want to carry it anymore. Father, take this spirit of bitterness from me and replace it with love, joy, and a sound mind, in Jesus' name. Amen.

Rebellion

Did you ever get your temper up and flatly refuse to do something you knew you should do? Of course! Children are great examples of this behavior. No one can forget the "terrible twos," when a child rebels against almost everything. Has God ever told His children to do something and had them rebel openly? Of course! The Bible has many examples. His children have not changed. We, His children, are constantly fighting to obey appropriately and not rebel or refuse His direction.

"I refuse to do what he tells me to do." "I'm not going to do what she tells me to do!" Sound familiar?

A gentleman came to a service and got delivered from smoking. He admitted that he didn't really like smoking anymore; however, he had continued to smoke because it irritated his spouse. They both got delivered from smoking and from the spirit of rebellion. Their lives changed.

Smoking was a symptom. Rebellion was the root. When he repented of the spirit of rebellion, the desire to smoke left. Often, when we deal with the root of rebellion, everything else falls into place, as well. If this is your problem, or if you are ministering to someone who has a problem with smoking, repentance for the spirit of rebellion is highly recommended.

Father, in the name of Jesus, I repent of the spirit of rebellion. It is sin. Take it from me. Put it on the cross, never to be held against me again, in Jesus' name. Amen.

Abuse

Where does abuse begin? Whether verbal, physical, or emotional, abuse is a characteristic of the fallen nature of man. It is also a characteristic of Satan.

Why do people put others down to build themselves up? Sometimes, it is because of insecurity, inferiority, frustration, feelings of inadequacy, sickness, or possibly the result of ancestral sins that have been passed down from generation to generation. Regardless of the root of the problem, it can be broken off from a life in the name of Jesus Christ.

I give you the authority to trample on serpents and scorpions, and

*over all the power of the enemy, and nothing shall by any means hurt
you.* (Luke 10:19)

People who were physically and verbally abused as children can repeat the same behavior with their children and with other people. They can become uncontrollably agitated and strike out unexpectedly at innocent people around them. The cruelty of a father, mother, or other person is not an excuse for the victim to be abusive of another. Jesus has given us a way to escape. The cycle can be broken.

If abuse seems to be a repetitive cycle in your family, stand in the gap and ask God to forgive your rebellious ancestors for their sins. They were acting against the laws in God's Word. The problem can be—and often is—a generational curse.

> Father, I repent of my sins, the sins of my rebellious ancestors, and of our sins of iniquity toward You and toward other people. In the name of Jesus, I cut the ancestral cord of iniquity from every family member since his or her generation, including myself and my children. This generational curse is now broken off of me and my children. Thank You, Father, in Jesus' name. Amen.

Occult Objects and Demonic Materials

An elderly lady was suffering from many illnesses and debilitating symptoms. While her regular physician was out of town, his replacement came to visit. A believer who loved to share her faith, this woman gave some Christian books to the new physician. In turn, he gave her some books on his religion, Islam.

Suddenly, her health took a nosedive. Weeks later, a family member found the books and DVD. After some reflection about the events that occurred, he determined that the day the books on Islam were brought into her room was the same day her health took a turn for the worse. Heart problems, infection, a small stroke, and a decline in mental acuity all appeared suddenly. The books and DVD were discovered and placed in a dumpster. The lady has had a great recovery and is back to normal health.

A naval officer and his wife were stationed in Cuba. They had experienced problems for many years and finally separated. During this separation, the wife met Jesus, and she stood in prayer and faith for her husband's salvation and the total restoration of their marriage. She wanted God's perfect will for her life. During this time of spiritual growth, she learned about the negative certain objects within her home. She destroyed all of them, and God brought her husband back home, where he was turned on to Jesus, too. They served Jesus together for years until the husband's death.

Another friend shared her experience with a similar situation. Her husband had received a gift from his daughter, who resided in another state. His ex-wife and her family actively participated in a cult. While driving down the highway one day, he suddenly developed tunnel vision. In other words, his vision was cut down to about one-third of its normal capability.

Thinking he was having a stroke, he immediately went to a doctor. Numerous tests were performed, and nothing was found. The only thing the doctor could suggest was a possible seizure, and he put this man on an antiseizure medication. Due to the drug's side effects, he couldn't drive or work. After much prayer, it was revealed that the "gift" had been brought into their bedroom the night before the tunnel vision developed, and it had carried a curse from the cult. He immediately took the gift outside and burned it. All the symptoms disappeared.

Look around your home. Be sure that you have no symbols of other gods hidden away. Oujia boards, statues of Buddha, devils, occult materials, or books about any of these things can cause havoc in your home. Check the movies, books, or music you and your family members may have brought into your immediate environment. They could have been brought in before you were saved or left by an overnight visitor. Whether the object is a family heirloom or a treasured gift from a special friend, you must get rid of it. Clean your house.

You have two houses to deal with: the physical home in which you live; and your body, in which your spirit and soul live.

Pray wisdom and protection over your home, your family members, your pets, your cars, and so forth. Plead the protection of the blood of Jesus over everything. Surround yourself with positive images and blessed objects. Listen to good music. Watch good movies. Read good books. Remember the question about things that edify, exhort, correct in love, or confirm? Choose to surround yourself with people who build you up with positive words, and surround yourself with objects that do the same.

You have two houses to deal with: the physical home in which you live; and your body, in which your spirit and soul live. It is up to you to both examine and choose either curses or blessings in all areas of your life.

Go through your house with prayer. Ask God to show you if there is anything you need to remove from your environment. Home should be a haven of rest and peace. Our homes should be the safest places we can be—places where we can be nourished, strengthened, and loved unconditionally. It is our responsibility to choose our homes wisely, protect our families from evil, and maintain our sanctuaries of love and peace. Satan has subtle ways of destroying what is good. Be wise and sensitive to his wiles. If your house doesn't bring you peace, pray that God will show you the cause.

Spiritual contamination can be more destructive than any dirt on the floor. Ask God to show you the true condition of your heart. Allow Him to be the Lord of your whole heart. He will show you events from your past hidden in the deepest crevices of your being. Handle them with God's help.

They say that you are what you eat. That saying refers to physical food, but it is also true regarding spiritual food. Eat well. Think well. When you are attracted to another individual, whether as a potential friend or a mate, consider this quote by Max Lucado: "A woman's heart should be so hidden in God that a man has to seek Him just to find her."

The Laying On of Hands

Many times, in our eagerness to be anointed, we run to the evangelist to have him lay hands on us—and later discover that he was not entirely sold out to God, or that he had backslidden into an ungodly lifestyle. Even those in cults believe in prayer—they are just not praying to the heavenly Father who alone is worthy of our devotion.

Many people want to lay hands on me and pray for me, but unless I know the people and their backgrounds, I normally do not let them lay hands on me. Spiritual things can be transferred between people. I choose to protect my environment and my anointing. Just because people want to lay hands on you and pray for you does not mean that you have to accept and receive their words, prayers, or actions. Again, you have a choice.

Have you ever had someone lay hands on you and then later wished that you had not let it happen? Many of us have. I have prayed the following prayer over myself several times, and I will pray it again when I feel the need to do so.

Father, many people have laid hands on me. Some have been good, and some have not been good. Father, I ask You to take anything that has been transferred to me that is not of You. I want only Your wisdom and Your Spirit working around and within me. In Jesus' name, amen.

Keep your house and heart clean.

CHAPTER 8

Can I Truly Forgive?

Your life can be changed permanently by studying and putting into practice the material covered in this chapter. You might even get a face-lift. Imagine a teaching that will make you look younger!

We all face unpleasant experiences, but we have to deal with them and survive to live another day. Difficult experiences make us who we are. Such experiences have given me the strength I need to get through life.

Somebody once asked, "Have you always been this strong?" The answer is *no*. In order to survive, somebody had to be the weak one in the family. My older brother is just like my mother—very, very strong willed. I would let them hash it out while I sat in the corner as the little, wimpy, weak one.

When God wanted to raise me up, I had to go through some very unpleasant experiences to become who I am today—a strong woman who will not sit in a corner anymore. God used the adversities in my life to make me stronger. I stood up to be counted. The protective, fighting mother in me came out in full force. It is amazing what you'll do for your children to survive. Once I found out who I was, I was able to face anything and everything that came my way. In order to fight the ultimate battle, I became a soldier, knowing that I would get through it victoriously because of God.

One of the first battles I had to deal with was unforgiveness.

Unforgiveness

Unforgiveness. Where does it come from? How does it develop? Do we learn it from parents or friends? Do we learn by example? When do its slithering tentacles imbed themselves in a heart or mind? Unforgiveness can poison and destroy every area of life—physical, emotional, mental, spiritual, and financial.

Perhaps immature parents don't know how to nurture their children. Instead of speaking words of kind, loving encouragement, some parents use negative words of derision that damage the impressionable mind and tender emotions of a child. The child then strikes out in fear and pain toward the smaller child next door, who then beats up the next vulnerable person or animal in the pecking order.

Usually, when retaliations are poured out on those who don't deserve them, confusion and pain spread like contagious diseases. Today, a lot of blame is focused on dysfunctional families, and many issues can be traced back to early problematic relationships within the family tree. Family members do play an important part, but friends, neighbors, teachers, schoolmates, and every person contacted during the day all contribute, as well. Some of these figures may bring peace, but others, if allowed, will ruffle feathers. Generally, people react in ways that they have found effective in protecting them from pain, based on past experiences.

All humans are born with a selfish nature. Everyone wants his or her own way and will cry until someone fixes things. Through thousands of tests, children quickly learn whom they can trust, whom they can talk back to, whom they can yell at or hit, and whom they can safely release their anger toward. Broken toys may be strewn all over the house by the end of a frustrating day.

As parents console their "victimized" children, platitudes such as, "They didn't really mean it" don't take away the pain. Parents often don't have the answers, and they usually don't train their children to handle the frustration of not getting their own way. All humans need to learn how to handle their

Venting in a healthy manner, knowing right from wrong, discipline, and not demanding instant gratification all must be taught by parents.

frustrations, pain, and anger. Venting in a healthy manner, knowing right from wrong, discipline, and not demanding instant gratification all must be taught by parents.

A friend of mine spent hours at the piano during her younger years. Her parents could tell what kind of a day she had experienced just by listening to her play. Bad days and their frustrations brought out loud, energetic music. Good days brought out more peaceful strains. She still releases many of her emotions at the keyboard. Unknowingly, she found an outlet that doesn't hurt anyone or cause damage to others. In fact, she has helped many others find peace through her music.

How do you handle your frustrations? We all welcome positive comments and get irritated with criticism. It is important to remember that life is never all positive; it is never all sweetness and love. We face all kinds of unexpected things every day. Each of us has to learn how to handle all types of situations. Some people run, lift weights, visit the batting cage, or attack a punching bag. Unfortunately, most don't know how to defuse their emotions in a healthy manner. Instead, they physically abuse another person or verbally lash out at whoever is nearby. Feelings of resentment, despair, insecurity, worthlessness, and depression are allowed to bloom and grow. I have not only witnessed these things; I am also able to speak from painful personal experience.

How do you handle the bad things, the negative comments, or the unpleasant criticisms? Do you take those things personally? Do you believe the negative, degrading comments thrown your way? Do you look behind the slurs? Can you consider the possibility that the negative comments are a lie? Can you understand that the person who said those things was having a bad day and struck out at you instead of at the true cause of her problem?

You Have a Choice

Choices. We are faced with thousands of them every day, from the moment we wake up until the time we fall asleep. We choose to either accept or reject every incident and word.

Too much negativity destroys. Too much praise develops pride, which always ends in destruction. (See Proverbs 16:18.) There has to be a balance.

A child learns by watching parents, friends, teachers, and others within his environment. What do your spiritual or physical children learn from you? Do they learn to forgive and forget? Do they learn to retaliate against the next person in their paths? Can they recognize that most negative effects aren't to be taken personally and instead can simply be ignored, forgiven, and forgotten?

Many people say that negative comments, anger, and frustration are from the enemy. Blame is assigned, but it is not always assigned with complete accuracy. Yes, the enemy has his effects; he whispers his suggestions to your mind. But it is your choice whether to accept and act on those suggestions. People do have to accept responsibility for their human actions and reactions.

More damage is caused in the body of Christ by unforgiveness than by anything else. I see it aging people as it opens the door for arthritis to enter. I ministered to a lady a few years ago who called me on the phone after seeing me on television. She listed all her problems and concluded with, "I can't even leave my home or my car because everything around me has to be so clean and purified. Even going to my neighbor's house has the potential of killing me. I can't come to your meeting. I can't go into a church or a hotel."

I told her that I would be happy to minister to her when I was in her city, and she agreed. She drove up in her car before the meeting started, and we sat in her backseat while her husband and a ministry partner sat in the front. The first question she asked was, "Why am I the one that is so sick when *he* is the one who did this to me?"

The night before their wedding, her husband-to-be did something that he had promised he would never do. He had apologized to her, repented, and asked her to forgive him. She said that she forgave him; however, throughout ten years of marriage, she went on hating the fact that he had let her down and betrayed her, even though he had asked for forgiveness. He felt free; meanwhile, her unforgiveness was literally eating her up inside, destroying her physically and in every other area of her life. She was freed when we prayed together that night.

God's Word tells us to love others, control anger, be kind to one another, and live in peace. Thus, we know by His Word that it is possible to achieve such an attitude and life. However, we still have to choose to do it. How? How can we control our tempers and fight the battle to maintain positive lives of love? We must *study, learn,* and *choose.*

Study God's Word. Learn how He wants you to live, how He wants to work through you, and how He wants you to spread His Word and His love. Choose to follow Him. Choose to allow His love to flow through you to others. Teach others by example.

Does your child, spouse, or friend know that he or she is accepted and loved unconditionally? Do you love those people with God's love? Only with Him living inside of you can you truly love others unconditionally. Only by seeking His face and heart can you react to all situations with His peace and joy.

What goes in is what comes out. A child cannot understand love unless he has received it from a parent or another adult. When a person hasn't received love and positive reinforcement from someone in his life, where does he learn what he should do? If you or someone you minister to needs this information, keep reading.

You can't show others God's love unless you allow Him to come into your life and love you first.

You can't show others God's love unless you allow Him to come into your life and love you first. You are going to have a very hard time showing anyone else mercy unless you understand the mercy God freely gives to you. Humans learn by example and by experience. Just as parents are tested by their children, God asks us to test Him. (See Malachi 3:10.)

Are you ready to love like He loves? Are you ready to let the scales fall from your eyes? Are you ready to look at God's children like He looks at them? They are all His special creations. We are all His children; we are all brothers and sisters. We should care about one another. We should cry with and for one another. More than anything, we should love one another. We should forgive one another. I am not perfect. You are not perfect. The people who have hurt us in the past are not perfect. We have all made mistakes. We have all been short with someone who didn't deserve it. We have all spoken in a moment of frustration or anger without thinking about how our words would affect or hurt the other person.

When you walk in the opposite of love, you walk in fear: fear that someone doesn't like you; fear that someone doesn't love you; fear that you have made another mistake and are going to experience someone's wrath, anger, or punishment...again; fear of rejection by someone who loves you—whether a spouse, a child, or a friend.

We are told to forgive others when they hurt us. Can you do that? Did they plan to hurt you? Did they stay up all night to plan out the bad things they would say to you? Probably not. But too often, we take all those negative things to heart and allow the pain to develop into resentment and unforgiveness.

Pain leads to stress. Stress causes the blood pressure to rise, often to unhealthy levels. High blood pressure damages the heart and the kidneys. Heart attacks, strokes, and diabetes are diagnosed. Stress and the accompanying tension cause the muscles and ligaments of the musculoskeletal system to tighten, cramp, and malfunction. Then, excess stomach acid pours into the stomach, causing irritation to the stomach lining and resulting in ulcers. This agitation of the digestive system can cause all kinds of difficulty in the intestines. Dietary upsets affect the body's nutrition, which, in turn, affects all areas of the body—mentally and physically.

The body attempts to cure itself, but the body's responses to outside influences continue. Illness or disease is diagnosed. More tension develops, followed by more stress. Costly treatments require more money, which leads to more tension. Medicines have side effects that are treated with more medicines, which cause more side effects.

Does this sound like a vicious circle? It is. It is a destructive cycle that leads to death. But we do have a choice. We can learn to recognize the negative influences on our spiritual, physical, and emotional lives. We can choose.

When a negative comment comes your way, you can choose to forgive and forget it. When a coworker does something to undermine your new project, you can choose to forgive and help that person reach his or her goal. When a spouse or a child says something that feels like a knife twisting in your back, you can choose to love that person unconditionally, regardless of his words or actions.

Forgive to Be Forgiven

> **Unforgiveness is the poison we drink, hoping that the other person will get sick.**

We need to forgive in order to maintain our bodily health and live in peace. We must forgive in obedience to God and His instructions in His Word. Unforgiveness is the poison we drink, hoping that the other person will get sick.

I don't want to poison my life with unforgiveness. I don't want to destroy my life and change everything I am doing or the direction in which I am going. Because unforgiveness causes a person to make bad decisions, it can influence you negatively until you gain freedom. And "*if the Son makes you free, you shall be free indeed*" (John 8:36). We have to fight to get rid of the chains that bind us in every area of our lives. We have to be free to go on with Him.

Unforgiveness can affect every area of your life. In addition to your health, your finances, and your prayer life, even your relationship with God can be affected. Note that I said "can affect." Unforgiveness doesn't *have* to affect your life. You have the ultimate choice.

Jesus has given us the perfect example of forgiveness. While He was still on the cross, He forgave His enemies—even though they did not deserve it. Let's search the Scriptures for His wisdom.

Jesus said, "Father, forgive them, for they do not know what they do." And they divided His garments and cast lots. (Luke 23:34)

Above all else, guard your heart, for it is the wellspring of life. (Proverbs 4:23 NIV)

Whenever you stand praying, if you have anything against anyone, forgive him, that your Father in heaven may also forgive you your trespasses. (Mark 11:25)

Let all bitterness, wrath, anger, clamor, and evil speaking be put away from you, with all malice. And be kind to one another, tenderhearted, forgiving one another, just as God in Christ forgave you. (Ephesians 4:31–32)

Our Father in heaven, hallowed be Your name. Your kingdom come. Your will be done on earth as it is in heaven. Give us this day our daily bread. And forgive us our debts, as we forgive our debtors. And do not lead us into temptation, but deliver us from the evil one. For Yours is the kingdom and the power and the glory forever. Amen. (Matthew 6:9–13)

If you forgive men their trespasses, your heavenly Father will also forgive you. But if you do not forgive men their trespasses, neither will your Father forgive your trespasses. (Matthew 6:14–15)

Bearing with one another, and forgiving one another, if anyone has a complaint against another; even as Christ forgave you, so you also must do. (Colossians 3:13)

Judge not, and you shall not be judged. Condemn not, and you shall

97

not be condemned. Forgive, and you will be forgiven. Give, and it will be given to you: good measure, pressed down, shaken together, and running over will be put into your bosom. For with the same measure that you use, it will be measured back to you.

(Luke 6:37–38)

Then Peter came to Him and said, "Lord, how often shall my brother sin against me, and I forgive him? Up to seven times?" Jesus said to him, "I do not say to you, up to seven times, but up to seventy times seven." (Matthew 18:21–22)

Notice how many Scriptures have conditions on our own forgiveness! We must forgive to be forgiven.

How Do I Know if I Need to Forgive Someone?

Some people use Matthew 18:21–22 as an excuse to continue hurting someone time and again. Their philosophy seems to be, *You have to forgive me.* This attitude traps the victim in a "doormat" mentality. Others continuously trample on the doormat. I was a doormat once, and I had to forgive many, many times. I know that people took advantage of me. Eventually, I discovered that being a Christian did not mean I had to be weak, stomped on, and abused. I could set boundaries. I could survive.

Personally, if I am having a problem with another person, I can feel it in my stomach. If I think about that person, my stomach feels funny. In fact, it just feels bad.

Think of someone who has hurt you. Do your thoughts suddenly have a sobering effect on your mood? Does your heart beat faster or harder? Does your stomach feel different? Is there a bad feeling deep within you? Has your peace left you? Do thoughts of that person distract you from your current purpose or actions? Do they bring related thoughts of self-doubt, self-incrimination, confusion, and other such accusations against your mind?

When you remember someone from your past, whether from yesterday or twenty years ago, do you feel good? Or do your thoughts cause you uneasiness? Does your stomach feel tense or nervous? Does a headache start to develop? Think of that person. Is there a bad feeling somewhere inside? Do you suddenly become obsessed with that incident? Do you replay the incident over and over in minute detail?

What if you were to suddenly run into that person today? Could you welcome her with your joy, peace, and love? Or does the thought of retaliation raise its ugly head? If that person called you today, could you welcome him into your life without pain or fear?

You don't remember doing anything bad to that person. You don't understand why he suddenly turned against you after you had done your best to help him. You certainly did not deserve her wrath, her negative comments, or her lies.

From your standpoint, it seems like this person is battling you personally. And that actually may be true. Too often, however, a rift in a relationship is caused by a misunderstanding or a wrong interpretation of the facts.

The old adage goes, *There are two sides to every story.* When several people witness the same event, they will explain their experiences from their own points of view. Often, the details are so different that one wonders if they are even describing the same event. They explain what they saw and understood from their own standpoints. Since we interpret events through the variety of previous experiences in our lives, our conclusions or beliefs may be based on incomplete or biased information.

Just like two people from different countries have to be patient until they actually understand each other's language, people from different backgrounds have to learn to communicate so they can truly understand each other, as well. A particular word or phrase in one area of a country may have an entirely different meaning in another area. Even though the widespread communication we enjoy through television and the Internet has done much to remove these differences, there are still barriers to communication.

For instance, two people may both be speaking English, but they

Unforgiveness is a type of bondage. It isolates, paralyzes, and destroys.

won't understand each other. An innocent comment may be misinterpreted, and someone will get insulted or hurt. Unforgiveness enters and slowly wraps its tentacles around every area of the individual's life.

Unforgiveness is a type of bondage. It isolates, paralyzes, and destroys. Slowly but surely, like a malignant, cancerous growth, it kills. Who is its originator? The enemy, of course. He doesn't want unity because there is power in unity of spirit. He will use anything to divide and conquer. What causes marriages to break up? What causes division in families? Confusion, misinterpretation of words or actions, lack of communication, fear, and unforgiveness. The enemy whispers lies into your mind to instigate and intensify problems. As we discussed earlier, actual physical bondage results from the emotional bondage of unforgiveness.

Do you have anyone you need to forgive? Do you have a hidden area in your heart that no one knows about? Have you hidden that hurt, that insult, so far away that no one else even knows about it?

I'm not advocating that you think back on everyone you have ever met and drudge up all the bad things you have ever experienced. Just understand that everyone has experienced negative things. How you react to those events makes the difference.

Have you ever known someone who appeared to have two sides to his personality? One time you see him, and he is full of love and fun; your next encounter is nothing but pain, frustration, and evil. The next, peace and love have returned. What is going on?

You have a choice to make every day. Whom will you listen to today? It is a daily choice, not just a onetime decision.

If it seems evil to you to serve the LORD, choose for yourselves this day whom you will serve, whether the gods which your fathers served that were on the other side of the River, or the gods of the Amorites, in whose land you dwell. But as for me and my house, we will serve the LORD. (Joshua 24:15)

People would tell me, "You need to forgive him. You need to forgive her." You probably have heard the same from well-meaning friends, but how should you go about following their advice? You could get up every morning, saying, "I forgive that person in the name of Jesus," but unless that person hurts you every day, you haven't truly forgiven him or her. The insult or hurt is still there, irritating you and distracting you from important tasks.

You must recognize that these negative words, these attacks of the devil, are meant to distract you from your calling and divert your attention away from your purpose. Turn to Jesus, the Holy Spirit, and your heavenly Father for help. Handle the situation with His wisdom, not yours.

Understand that we hurt God every day of our lives. We are disobedient. We aren't in His perfect will every minute of the day—far from it. As long as you call yourself human, you are not and never will be perfect. You and I need God's forgiveness for our shortcomings and mistakes every single day. We can try and try and try, but we will always mess up and require His merciful forgiveness.

Many times, the thoughtless person who wronged you doesn't deserve to be forgiven. Well, you don't, either. Through His grace, God will forgive you. Since we are instructed to be like God (see Ephesians 5:1–2), we need to forgive others just as God forgives us. Are others going to feel any better when you forgive them? No. Are they going to know that you forgave them? No. Are *you* going to feel better? Oh, yes!

> **God wants to free you in every area of your life by breaking the chains that hold you in bondage.**

God wants to free you in every area of your life by breaking the chains that hold you in bondage. Many people come to services hunched over with their heads down and their faces hidden behind their hair. They appear totally dejected, depressed, and downtrodden. After just one session of ministry, though, these same people look entirely different. Their heads are up, their shoulders are back, and their chins are high. They appear strong again because the weight of unforgiveness and word curses has been broken off of them.

Slowly but surely, too many people allow abusive situations to wear them down to nothing, to total immobility. I refused to allow the enemy to keep me in bondage once I knew how to get free.

How many times do you need to ask God through Jesus Christ to forgive sin? If you commit one sin, one request for forgiveness covers it. One request equals forgiveness for that incident. Unfortunately, we aren't perfect. Sometimes, we forget all our little slipups during the day and have to ask forgiveness for many things at one time. Still, one request for forgiveness is enough. God says that He doesn't remember our sins once we have asked His forgiveness (see Jeremiah 31:34), so bringing up the same infidelity time after time is a waste of your time and His.

So, I ask again: *How many times do you need to ask God through Jesus Christ to forgive sin?* Once!

If we fail to find it in our hearts to forgive others around us, how can we expect God to forgive us? We must look to His forgiveness as the ultimate example for our actions. We don't deserve His forgiveness, but He freely gives it. Think about it: when they repent, He also freely forgives those who hurt us. Just as we don't deserve that forgiveness, those people don't, either. However, God forgives us all. Have you ever hurt anyone? Certainly, you have. We all have. Maybe not intentionally with malice, but we have all experienced misunderstandings—whether as givers or as recipients.

The enemy is constantly making suggestions to our minds. We have to choose our reactions.

A wonderful Christian lady in Minnesota found out that her sixteen-year-old daughter was pregnant. She explained that her first reactions were anger, frustration, and fear. She wanted to lash out with derision, condemnation, and judgment. In the midst of a tearful confession, her daughter explained that she had been to the altar at church to ask for God's forgiveness. The mother wisely realized that if God had already forgiven her wayward daughter, then who was she to judge and condemn? She chose to love and forgive like Jesus does.

What would Jesus do with your situation? What should I do with mine? What should you do? Choose life—God's life of peace and love. No one else can make that choice for you. You have to make it for yourself.

All God wants is a willing heart. Do you want to walk in His love? Ask for it. Do you want to walk in His mercy? Ask for it. Do you want total, unconditional forgiveness for your sins? Ask for it. God separates our sins from us when we choose to put our sins at the foot of the cross of Jesus. And with His love, mercy, and compassion working in and through us, we can freely love and forgive others, just as He has forgiven us.

Don't wait. Choose now. And remember that unforgiveness is sin. It will separate you from God.

Unforgiveness is sin. It will separate you from God.

God doesn't cleanse the sin itself; He cleanses people. He separates the sin from us and puts it on the cross of Jesus Christ, never to be remembered again. God sacrificed His only begotten Son to pay the ultimate price for our sins.

If there is any doubt in your mind about whether or not you have forgiven others, speak forgiveness now. Speak forgiveness toward anyone you believe has hurt you. Not forgiving them is not hurting them at all. You are only hurting yourself. Again, it is your choice. Do you want to stay trapped in pain, anger, and fear? Do you want to stay trapped in unforgiveness?

Unwind the tentacles of unforgiveness from your heart. Destroy those works of the enemy. You have the keys to be *free!* What is your goal? Choose freedom!

Forgiveness Versus Unforgiveness

A lady in Tulsa came to the altar after hearing my teaching on unforgiveness. She had suffered with painful arthritis for many years. Her healing came instantaneously after she forgave.

Earlier in this chapter, I told the story of a different woman who came asking the question, "Why am I sick when *he* is the one that did that horrible thing to me?"

Again, what that person did to her was wrong—and it will always be wrong—but God will handle the situation. *"'Vengeance is Mine, I will repay,' says the Lord"* (Hebrews 10:30). You must forgive the person who wronged you as God forgives you, with complete faith that God will manage the situation without your help or interference. We have to believe in His Word and leave it in His hands.

In a meeting in Northern Ireland, a lady scared everyone by screaming out, "I can't forgive him!" We prayed, and she was set free from unforgiveness toward her ex-husband.

If we aren't willing, we won't be forgiven, either. Burdened with unforgiveness, we may feel tired and exhausted. As I mentioned in chapter seven, many people describe a feeling of lightness after we minister to them. After forgiveness, the burden and the pain are gone. Everyone has to be willing to forgive.

Once again, forgiveness does not mean that what the other person did is now okay, but forgiveness sets you *free*. You can choose to break the bondage of the enemy. You can choose to be free and to return to God's perfect will. *"Choose for yourselves this day whom you will serve"* (Joshua 24:15).

Only God can separate us from the sin of unforgiveness. Go to the cross. Place your unforgiveness at the feet of Jesus. Receive His forgiveness and allow Him to heal you!

How do you minister to someone who needs to forgive? Listen to the Lord. He will give you words to say—words of knowledge. You don't need the minute details of any situation. Forgiveness covers a multitude of situations.

There is a mirror on the wall in our office. After we minister to people, we ask them to look in the mirror. They may or may not be crying; however, even through tears, they will look ten years younger. They are free; they are not carrying the burdens anymore. The chains of bondage have been destroyed.

I will share one more revelation for those of you who want to be free. God takes our tears and puts them in a bottle. (See Psalm 56:8.) This is meant for both men and women, because the Bible does not say that only women can cry, or that only women's tears are stored by God.

I asked God one day, "Why are You saving all of my tears?" I thought that was kind of strange.

He replied through the Holy Spirit, "I am saving them for restoration, and I am keeping count. For every tear sown in sorrow, you will reap as much in tears of joy."

Grab some tissues or a handkerchief and continue with this prayer.

Father, what _____ did to me was sin, and it hurt me deeply. I forgive this person. Separate this sin from _____ and put it on the cross. On the day of judgment, hold no accusations against ___ for those sins. Father, bless _____!

You may need to repeat the last sentence of that prayer a few times. List all those whom you need to forgive, and repeat the prayer for each person on your list. You may want to include some or all of the following:

MOTHER	FATHER	BROTHER
SISTER	SPOUSE	EX-SPOUSE
BOSS	PASTOR	SPOUSE
CHILDREN	FRIEND	COWORKER

If you forgive the sins of any, they are forgiven them; if you retain the sins of any, they are retained. (John 20:23)

"To Him all the prophets witness that, through His name, whoever believes in Him will receive remission of sins." While Peter was still

105

speaking these words, the Holy Spirit fell upon all those who heard the word.   (Acts 10:43–44)

Finally, brothers, whatever is true, whatever is noble, whatever is right, whatever is pure, whatever is lovely, whatever is admirable— if anything is excellent or praiseworthy—think about such things.
(Philippians 4:8 NIV)

After ministry, someone came up to me with eyes still moistened with tears and said, "I didn't know forgiveness would feel this good."

CHAPTER 9

Dealing with Stress, Trauma, and Depression

S tress, pressure, worry—these things affect our lives on a daily basis. Our reactions to stressors will determine whether the effects are temporary or long lasting. We can either claim the problems and suffer or choose to give all the issues and headaches of life to God, who is capable of solving all our problems.

We don't have all the answers, but we know who does. We can't solve the problems of the world; however, we know who can. We don't understand the path He has chosen for us, but He knows His perfect will for each of us. We don't know where to walk, but He will tell us when and where to take our next steps.

Saying words is easier than taking action. What do we have to do? And how do we do it? *Nothing alters until you put it on the altar.* In other words, nothing will ever change unless you give it to God.

> **Nothing alters until you put it on the altar.**

Overcoming Fear

There is no fear in love; but perfect love casts out fear, because fear involves torment. But he who fears has not been made perfect in love. We love Him because He first loved us. If someone says, "I love God," and hates his brother, he is a liar; for he who does not love his brother whom he has seen, how can he love God whom he has not seen? And this commandment we have from Him: that he who loves God must love his brother also. (1 John 4:18–21)

The Word of God says that there is no fear in love. The opposite of

> **I don't want the enemy to win. I want perfect love to be in my heart always, and I want all fear to be gone.**

love is fear—not hatred, but fear. When you have fear, it is not from God, because God is love.

Years ago, I told God, "It seems like the enemy is going after the hearts and emotions of people to destroy families and homes." Through prayer and revelation, God revealed that He is love. Satan is going to attack us where we're most vulnerable—our hearts. If he can get us to question our love of God and turn against our families, he has won. If the enemy can destroy us emotionally, he wins.

I don't want him to win. I want perfect love to be in my heart always, and I want all fear to be gone.

Sometimes, my husband travels with me. When he is not traveling with me, however, I have total confidence in him and in what he is doing. If I am gone for a week, he spends one or two nights out with the boys—his boys. He has four sons. The rest of the time, he's at home studying, reading, praying, worshipping, and staying up most the night with the Lord. When he falls asleep, the only thing in bed with him is his Bible, because he falls asleep while reading, thinking, and meditating on God's Word.

This gives me immense peace. I have no fear that he is out doing something that he shouldn't be doing.

Overcoming Stress

Give all your worries and cares to God, for he cares about you.
(1 Peter 5:7 NLT)

Stress will bring about many diseases. A few of them include irritable bowel syndrome, high blood pressure, stomach ulcers, acid reflux disease, strokes, migraines, and arthritis. Handling stress is a choice. You don't have to worry about anything. God has told us that He will take care of all our problems.

Have you ever tried to fix your spouse or your children? Several years ago, I was trying to help my children survive the trauma that had attacked our home and family. They were faced with numerous opportunities to overcome. They each responded differently to the pain. I tried everything to fix them and make them better. The more I tried to bring them to church, the more some of them rebelled.

Utter frustration was making me sick. Sleep was impossible because I didn't know what my children were doing or what time they were coming in at night. The mother in me was worried—even about the older children. They would come home and describe where they had gone and what they had done.

Inside, I was screaming, "Who are these children? Have they forgotten everything they learned about God?" The more I told them, the more they went in the other direction.

One day, I fell to my knees and cried out, "God, I can't fix them! I can't heal their hurts! I give them to You!"

He replied, "Really? I have been waiting for you to give them to Me. *You* have gotten in the way of My Holy Spirit."

I was trying to do God's work instead of allowing Him to be the Holy Spirit in their lives. When they returned from their next evening out, I simply said, "I hope you had a good evening. I'm going to bed now." They couldn't understand what had happened to me. Then, I went into my bathroom and said to my heavenly Father, "Did You see what *Your* daughters did?"

It is up to God to change the people around you. He is capable of handling all your issues.

When I took my hands off my children, they made their own choices to stop their rebellion. Their lives turned around, and they started serving God and going to church again. God has transformed them. He did a better job than I could have! If a conflict arises in your family or marriage, you can voice your opinion; however, it is up to God to change the people around you. Let the Holy Spirit handle the problem. He is capable of handling all your issues.

We all can feel like it is our job to fix our family members, whether children or spouses. We may feel like we have to be perfect with everything. But it is not our responsibility to "fix" our children or spouses. It is not our job to cram Jesus down their throats—they might throw up. It is our job to love them unconditionally.

When they get past the age of accountability, they are in God's hands, not ours. According to Jewish law, the age of accountability is thirteen. Up to thirteen years of age, a child's sins belong to the parents. After thirteen, a child is responsible for his or her own sins. In our society, the age of accountability varies with the child's level of maturity. Some may be mature at twelve while others may reach maturity at twenty-three.

> But the LORD says, "The captives of warriors will be released, and the plunder of tyrants will be retrieved. For I will fight those who fight you, and **I will save your children**."
>
> (Isaiah 49:25 NLT, emphasis added)

Forget the tension. Forget the worry. Forget the indigestion. You don't have to carry any of that on your shoulders, mind, or heart, because God's got it. How do you release it? Walk it out through prayer. *Nothing alters until you put it on the altar.*

Prayer for Releasing a Spouse

Father, You know that I have tried to fix my husband/wife. Lord, I lay _____ on your altar. I release _____ to You. I thank You for _____. Father, bless _____, and bless our marriage. Amen.

Prayer for Releasing Parents

Father, I lay my mom and dad on your altar. I don't understand some of the things they're doing. I know I can't fix them, so I release them to You, in Jesus' name. Father, bless them. Amen.

Prayer for Releasing Children

Father, I lay my child _____ on Your altar. I thank You for what You have done in _____'s life already, and I ask You to bless _____ in Jesus' name. I've done all I know to do as a mother/father, and I release _____ to You. Father, bless _____. Show me how to be a better mother/father. Amen.

Repeat this prayer individually for each of your children by name.

Often, when teaching on stress, I pick up a sturdy, upholstered chair and place it upside down on my head while I continue with my teaching. Sounds strange. Looks strange. However, the demonstration is never forgotten by those who see it. Everyone understands the principle by the time I release the chair and put it down.

I travel most of the time. My husband travels with me when he can, but he still has a very responsible position at his job. He often has to stay home while the ministry team flies off to fulfill God's call on our lives.

If I am away from him, whether overseas for an extended time or out of town for a few days, I have to make a choice. Do I worry about him? Do I wonder what he is doing? Whom is he spending time with? If I chose to worry, I would be carrying the weight of my husband on myself. I don't know about you, but it is really hard for me to teach with a heavy chair on my head. It is hard to minister when I'm carrying worry and stress on my shoulders.

In addition to my husband, I have four grown daughters (some of them married), a grandson, a granddaughter, four stepsons, and a worldwide healing ministry. I wouldn't be able to preach effectively if I was constantly thinking, *Are we going to make payroll? Are all the people doing their jobs? What about my husband, Kelley? Our children? Their finances?* My elderly parents are having frequent health challenges. I could choose to worry about them continuously or even cancel all my ministry dates to sit at their sides every day. However, I know that God has carried them through dozens of years of ministry, and He will continue to hold them in His hands.

A chair on my head obviously gets very heavy. Similarly, carrying all the worries about family and business affairs also gets heavy, as well as oppressive.

As you carry around all these worries and concerns, you start to wonder why you have a neck problem. You wonder why your shoulders hurt, not to mention your back. What are you carrying?

Ladies, our shoulders are barely strong enough to carry our purses, much less our husbands. Often, we choose to walk around carrying the weight of our finances on our shoulders; we carry the weight of our spouses, our families, and our children—especially if they are unsaved. And it is killing us.

God wants us to release those situations to Him. He wants us to give all our concerns and cares to Him. Let God carry them.

When someone comes to take the chair off my head during the demonstrations, relieving all the pressure and pain, I have to choose to release it. I could hold on to the chair (keep worrying about my family, friends, or business) with all my might, believing that I have the ability to fix things—my children, my husband, and everything around me.

> **If you release everything to God, life is much more fun.**

Instead, I choose to release the chair, just like I choose to release all my cares and concerns to God every day. If you release everything to God, life is much more fun. I don't have to worry about Kelley. I don't have to worry about any of the children. If I am doing what God wants me to do, it is His responsibility to take care of my husband, my children, my grandchildren, my parents, and the ministry. I've learned that I have to give everything and everyone to God. I can't fix my children. I can't fix my husband. I am called to love them unconditionally, and with the empowering presence of the Holy Spirit within me, I can do that willingly and with my whole heart.

What do you carry around with you? Trying to fix your spouse and practically killing yourself in the process is not going to do a bit of good. The more you try to correct other people, the more they will rebel against your efforts.

Who of you by worrying can add a single hour to his life?

(Matthew 6:27 NIV)

Finances

Some of you are in so much debt that you can't even see straight. I believe in doing whatever I can to be out of debt. I don't even like having a mortgage. The root word of *mortgage* is the same as the root word of *morgue*. Like a death sentence, it makes you think you are never going to get it paid off. You may live in a house for thirty years and still feel like you have another three hundred years worth of payments left.

How do you get out of debt? What's the first step? People say, "I give tithes and offerings." You'd better be doing that anyway! If you are not tithing, repent and start tithing. If you are not giving offerings, repent and start giving offerings. If you are spending foolishly, repent of foolish spending and stop. Monitor your finances and watch them turn around! Watch your indebtedness disappear. Healing in every area of our lives comes through repentance.

People's debts have been totally wiped out once they started following God's principles. Personally, my debts are wiped out. One couple had a debt of approximately $50,000 that they had dealt with for about eight years. They became partners with this ministry and explained that they wanted to be out of debt by the end of the year. They gave their offering. Within three days, they received a phone call from

Healing in every area of our lives comes through repentance.

a person who said, "God laid it on my heart to pay whatever you have left on your bill for that situation." Supernaturally, their debt of $50,000 was wiped out within one week. That's our God!

When you obediently follow through with what God has called you to do, you plant your seed (tithes, offerings, alms, money, time, energy, etc.) into different areas of ministry. Follow His guidance, and then watch what God will do with your finances. God is so amazing!

Repent, tithe, give offerings, and be obedient to when, where, and how He tells you to give. If you are burdened with a mountain of debt, remember that the Word of God says that *"whoever says to this mountain, 'Be removed and be cast into the sea'...will have whatever he says"* (Mark 11:23). Cut up the credit cards; pay everything in cash. If you have to use your credit cards, pay them off every month.

The stress of debt sometimes feels totally overwhelming. Loss of sleep, worry, a short temper, and calls from creditors all add to the pressure. If you are being obedient with your tithes, offerings, and alms, lay the rest of your debt at the Lord's feet. How? Pray.

> Father, I lay my finances on Your altar. I repent for any foolish spending and for the times I haven't tithed and given offerings. That's sin. Take this sin from me and put it on the cross. Your Word says in Philippians 4:19 that You are going to supply all of my needs according to Your riches in glory by Christ Jesus. I don't have to worry about the problem anymore. I know I have to do my part. I will tithe, give offerings, and stop spending foolishly. You, in turn, are going to bless me and take care of me. Thank You, Jesus. Amen.

Let me give you another example. It's a cute story that will further explain this principle.

When my daughter Charity and son-in-law Ted were expecting their first child, they talked about using cloth diapers. But after using one disposable diaper from the hospital, we discovered how wonderful they were. Disposable diapers are quite expensive, however, and Charity and Ted decided not to use them because of the cost.

When they explained their decision to me, I told them, "You're limiting God. You are trying to figure out in the natural how you are going to pay for the diapers instead of allowing God to meet your every need. One of your needs is diapers. I believe that God is going to supernaturally supply you with diapers."

Their response was, "Yeah, whatever, Mom." Some people believe that faith for such a simple thing is too far-fetched. Yet God cares about every area of our lives.

Two days later, somebody rang my daughter's doorbell. She and Ted opened the door to discover cases and cases of diapers on the doorstep. They did not have to buy any diapers the whole time my grandson had to wear them. They had diapers left over for his new sister, as well. Praise God, they have a lot of storage space!

I am not talking just about diapers. I am talking about God supplying your every need. God doesn't just supply. He's an overabundant type of God. What does God want? He wants a father spending quality time with his son, not having to work extra hours at a second job to pay for diapers. My grandson has had his dad with him every weekend, reading to him, playing with him, teaching him things, and loving him.

When your finances are placed on the altar, God will take care of you, even if your need includes diapers. The Bible says, *"my God shall supply all your need"* (Philippians 4:19, emphasis added).

When my grandson was born, I didn't have any baby supplies to use with him; what was I going to do when he came to visit? Guess what happened. Other than a nice car seat that I purchased, everything was given to me before Charity and Ted even arrived with their newborn son. I had a need because I had a grandbaby coming to visit me. I am now prepared for all my grandbabies' visits in the future.

> **When your finances are placed on the altar, God will take care of you.**

Because I have faithfully and regularly given my finances to the Lord, He has supplied. It isn't just Mom's faith and miracles anymore; my children are learning that they can put their finances on His altar and be amazed by His provisions. They are witnessing their own miracles from God.

We don't have to get stressed out over our finances. I like being happy; I don't like being worried. Worry brings wrinkles, ulcers, heart attacks, high blood pressure, and strokes. I choose not to worry. I give all those stressful things to God.

What is causing your stress? Have you given it to God? Sometimes, after a few weeks, your neck may start to hurt and your shoulders may start to ache. What do you do? First, ask yourself, *Did I sleep wrong?* Second, ask, *Did I pick up something off the altar that I had given to God?* If the answer is the latter, you know what to do. "Father, I can't fix my finances. In the name of Jesus, I lay them back on Your altar."

You may have to do this a few times before you learn to leave your worries at God's feet. Let Him take your concerns and handle them *all.* Let Him do all the "worrying." He is up all night anyway, so why should you be?

Don't limit God! If you don't have a house, just thank God for the house He is going to give you, which will be totally paid for. Take the limits off of God in every area of your life—financially, emotionally, spiritually, mentally—as well as in regard to your own abilities. Allow God to overwhelm you with blessings!

Trauma, Depression, and Hopelessness

Major trauma in your life can also bring on illnesses and disease. When you experience a major trauma, you must recognize what is happening and deal with the issues. You must also understand the implications of trauma when you are ministering to others.

An eighty-year-old woman came to me with complaints of fibromyalgia. When she was three years old, she had witnessed the murder of her eleven-year-old brother. After this horrific and traumatic

116

event, her body had started shutting down. She was attacked by both depression and unforgiveness that lasted most of her life. Together, we prayed for forgiveness and followed with a prayer to release her from the spirit of trauma and spirit of pain. The fibromyalgia disappeared.

Why are you sick? Are you battling a particular illness? Have you experienced serious trauma in your past?

When a traumatic event occurs in a person's life, fear enters. It first affects the heart and eventually the body. The person loses hope and fear grows. Fear opens up the door for depression. When nothing gets better, hope seems impossible, and the immune system deteriorates. The body starts producing stress hormones in response to the stress. When the endorphins (happy hormones) are not produced, sleep can either be impossible or become excessive. Drugs or alcohol can become havens to temporarily cover up the pain and hopelessness. Over a period of time, a person can have thoughts of suicide as the only option.

Who is in control in this scenario? Certainly not God! This vicious cycle has to be stopped at the very beginning. Whenever something traumatic happens to you, pray for the spirit of trauma to go. If someone comes to you for ministry and you identify a previous trauma in his or her life, pray for the spirit of trauma to go.

A spirit of trauma can be brought on by any traumatic or stressful experience. The list of possibilities is long: job loss, changing homes, moving to another city, separation from family, financial devastation, the loss of a house, the death of a family member or friend, a traffic accident, serious illness, a fall, a debilitating injury, divorce, the loss of a relationship, and so many others.

I have prayed for many people who then received partial healing. In many instances, following a prayer for the spirit of trauma to go, the person was dramatically healed the rest of the way.

Traumatic experiences and stress can lead to tiredness, depression, fibromyalgia, and chronic fatigue syndrome. Depression will impair your immune system. The immune system can attack itself or just shut down.

As I have been writing this book over the past year, I have learned the powerful effects of the spirit of trauma. Your heart remembers every instance of trauma that it has ever received or experienced. You must rid your life of the spirit of trauma, if it is present. Place your hand over your heart and repeat this prayer:

Father, in the name of Jesus, I command the spirit of trauma and fear to leave. Amen.

Jesus is our hope!

Many times, a person will actually feel something different in his or her heart after praying. *"Many are the afflictions of the righteous, but the LORD delivers him out of them all"* (Psalm 34:19). *"Hope deferred makes the heart sick, but when the desire comes, it is a tree of life"* (Proverbs 13:12). Jesus is our hope!

Many times in my life, I have felt like I was all alone and didn't know what I was going to do. Yet God was there with me every time. *"As I was with Moses, so I will be with you. I will not leave you nor forsake you. Be strong and of good courage"* (Joshua 1:5–6). *"In my distress I called to the LORD, and he answered me"* (Jonah 2:2 NIV).

Depression is brought on by hopelessness. As you dwell on hopelessness, it becomes oppression and then develops into depression. And it can get even worse from there. *"I sought the LORD, and He heard me, and delivered me from all my fears"* (Psalm 34:4). *"For God has not given us a spirit of fear, but of power and of love and of a sound mind"* (2 Timothy 1:7).

God wants us to maintain hope because He is our Hope. If you are weak and tired, remember that God is the Answer. How do you manage the stress? Where do you get the strength to face another day? The answers to all our questions are found in His Word!

Cast your burden on the LORD, and He shall sustain you.

(Psalm 55:22)

He gives power to the weak, and to those who have no might He increases strength. (Isaiah 40:29)

Do not sorrow, for the joy of the LORD is your strength.

(Nehemiah 8:10)

Let the weak say, "I am strong." (Joel 3:10)

Do not fret....Trust in the LORD....Commit your way to the LORD.... Rest in the LORD, and wait patiently for Him; do not fret because of him who prospers in his way, because of the man who brings wicked schemes to pass. (Psalm 37:1, 3, 5, 7)

Be anxious for nothing, but in everything by prayer and supplication, with thanksgiving, let your requests be made known to God; and the peace of God, which surpasses all understanding, will guard your hearts and minds through Christ Jesus. (Philippians 4:6–7)

Come to Me, all you who labor and are heavy laden, and I will give you rest. Take My yoke upon you and learn from Me, for I am gentle and lowly in heart, and you will find rest for your souls.

(Matthew 11:28–29)

Remember: Everything can alter when you lay it on His altar!

CHAPTER 10

Freedom from False Responsibility and Guilt

Guilt is another one of those heart issues that doesn't necessarily have outward manifestations of physical symptoms. Nevertheless, it can be part of the root cause of many physical ailments. I have been affected by guilt and have had to deal with its consequences. Thus, I am speaking from both personal experience and the perspective of a witness who has seen others freed from this rather obscure but very real form of bondage.

Another way to label the issue of guilt is "false responsibility" or "self-blame." People often blame themselves for something bad that has happened to themselves or to someone they love. Some examples are: a spouse or child dies; a loved one turns against his or her God-based training from childhood and embraces an alternate lifestyle or addiction; a bad decision causes an accident resulting in life-changing physical problems, disability, or injuries. In any case, some form of trauma occurs that is outside anyone's control, but a person blames himself, picking up and carrying the responsibility that does not belong to him.

God has laid a lot of things on my heart lately. Many of my recent experiences have taught me much about God's principles. I have seen many people healed since I received this revelation and started teaching on it. My prayer is that you, too, will be touched and set free by what you read.

Brethren, if a man is overtaken in any trespass, you who are spiritual restore such a one in a spirit of gentleness, considering yourself lest you also be tempted. Bear one another's burdens, and so fulfill the law of Christ. (Galatians 6:1–2)

120

This Scripture says that we are responsible for helping others and loving them. It doesn't say that we are responsible for their choices.

People give us things, and we accept the responsibility for those things without thinking. We have to be very careful about what we accept from other people. For instance, we are not to accept and take on another's responsibility.

I prayed with a certain lady about her husband. He was a leader in the church and an awesome man of God. After being married for more than thirty-five years, they were still madly in love with each other. Suddenly, he was diagnosed with a malignant brain tumor. He went into a coma and was hospitalized. We prayed, and he came home.

A short time later, it happened again. We prayed, and he started moving and opening his eyes. This woman trusted God to the very end for her husband's healing, but he died. Afterward, God spoke through one of her friends: "I had an unfair advantage. I showed him a glimpse of the other side. He chose to go home." There was nothing she could do but trust God.

When I saw this woman a few months later, I felt a spirit of grief and trauma on her. When I ministered to her, I told her exactly what she had been feeling: "You feel guilty that he died. You are thinking, *If I had been a better wife, if I had prayed harder, if I had called Joan one more time for prayer, he would still be alive.*" None of that was true, of course. She had been listening to the wrong voices. Guilt and shame are destructive forces. They do not originate with God. After prayer and ministry, this woman is now *free!*

Another story illustrates this point well. A beautiful baby girl was born to a friend of mine, and she was diagnosed with Down syndrome. Talking with the distraught mother, I identified the sneaky tentacles of guilt being entwined around her heart and mind. Her self-blame talk included: "If I had taken more of those supplements, if I had taken my prenatal vitamins, if I had quit work sooner, if I had rested more, then my baby would be healthy."

> **Anyone who listens to negative thoughts long enough will start to believe those thoughts.**

She had done nothing wrong. There was no blame to place on anyone. The condition was not related to anything she had done or not done. I ministered freedom and peace to her. God had given her a precious gift. He had trusted her and her husband with a very special child to care for and to love. Today, they are set *free!*

Anyone who listens to negative thoughts long enough will start to believe those thoughts. Imagine listening to such comments as these: "It's your fault. You are the one who did this. You caused this. You destroyed this person. You....You....You!" Restorative sleep eludes you. Your body reacts to both the lack of sleep and the tension from all the pressure. You can't think logically anymore.

Under this kind of painful existence, it is difficult to live a normal life. Your appetite is affected. You don't want to admit to your negative thoughts or ask for help. You believe that you deserve the pain and agony you are feeling. Eventually, you even cut off communication with God. You wonder, *How can He love me because of this terrible thing I've done?*

Some people experience complications with pregnancy, aren't able to get pregnant, or are unable to carry a child to full term. Their self-accusations might include, "God isn't giving me a child. He must believe I would be a bad mother. I must be getting punished for something I did in the past." Of course, you should examine yourself for possible problems, but after that point, you have to stop beating yourself up about it.

I asked a lady to help me explain this principle to a congregation. She believed that she had adjusted appropriately and was free from guilt regarding the birth of a mentally challenged child many years earlier. As I had her repeat the prayer to be set free from false responsibility, she suddenly started sobbing. She had mistakenly blamed herself for doing something to cause her child's problems. She was finally and completely set free from the guilt that she had been carrying.

Adopted children can also suffer from false responsibility. As they observe friends' happy families, thoughts like these often go through their minds: *I was so bad that my mother and father gave me up for adoption. They didn't want me. They threw me away like an old shoe. I must be very, very bad.*

What could an innocent baby do to cause a parent to give him or her up? Instead of feeling rejected by mothers who probably couldn't provide adequately for them at that time in their lives, adopted children should rejoice that they are special and chosen by parents who love them. No matter what happens with our earthly parents, God forever loves His children unconditionally.

Have You Been Believing a Lie?

Maybe you were the oldest child in your family. Perhaps a sudden death or serious illness thrust you into the role of caretaker, responsible for raising the younger children. Many children take on so much responsibility that is not theirs to take on. Children need time to be children; they grow up too fast as it is.

One time, I was praying for a lady in one of our meetings, and nothing seemed to be happening. Her abdominal pain would not go away. I knew that there had to be a deep-seated spiritual root behind this pain. It turned out that her father had dealt with emotional problems for years. When he would get depressed and feel suicidal, he would call her, and she would go over to sit with him.

One day, she wasn't home to receive his call. When she was able to retrieve her voice mails, she immediately went to see her father. She found him dead. Since that time, she had taken on the false responsibility for her father's suicide. She felt as if someone had punched her in the stomach. After ministry, her pain left instantly. She had come to the meeting in pain but left rejoicing and *free!*

Listen carefully. People often carry the burden of someone's death, a child's imperfection, a divorce, or some other catastrophe. They pick up and carry the burdens of blame for things outside their control. They did

Do not accept the negative. Welcome only the positive.

all they knew to do. Their logical minds knew the situations were not caused by anything they did or did not do. They have to release the guilt and shame by giving them to God. Do not accept the negative. Welcome only the positive.

In 2007, when my mother was in the hospital and at death's door numerous times, I had to choose to leave her in God's hands and continue with my ministry schedule. I was criticized for being a neglectful daughter because I didn't cancel everything and sit at her bedside every day.

When my parents were faced with their first health challenges, I was there much of the time. But God didn't call me to hold their hands. I could have stopped traveling and cared for them myself, but there are people trained specifically for that position who are much better qualified to care for my parents' needs than I. I am not trained to meet their health care needs. I had to learn to turn off those critical words and be comfortable letting others take care of my parents' personal and health needs.

Many people tried to heap guilt on me because they *thought* they knew what my mother would want me to do. If they had known my mother, they would have realized that she would have been very disappointed in me if I had cancelled God's work to hold her hand as she lay in the hospital.

My first responsibility is to God. My next responsibility is to my husband. I am not responsible to fulfill the call of God on my parents' lives. My responsibility is to do God's work, and while I am doing His work, His responsibility is to take care of my parents, my husband, my children, and everyone else I care about. God told me, "You take care of My business, and I will take care of yours." I have to obey God, not man.

People will press your guilt button. I used to be highly motivated by guilt. Through the years, my guilt button has been pushed countless times. I finally learned to turn it off. It's not even on "vibrate" anymore. I no longer accept any words of guilt. I will not accept false responsibility. It would interfere with God's call on my life, and I protect that precious calling.

"If you really loved God, you would do this." Have you ever heard something like that? Perhaps someone has told you, "If you loved me, you would do this or wouldn't do that." If words like that are the reason why you do or don't do something, you are motivated by guilt. You are being manipulated. In God's Word, such manipulation is considered a form of witchcraft.

Guilt from Molestation

Another sensitive issue that is part of this false sense of responsibility is molestation—whether physical, emotional, or sexual. If someone was molested as a child, he or she may suffer from self-blame and false responsibility for the entire incident. When I was four years old, I was molested by a male relative. If a trusted relative does the molesting, the child believes it must be normal. Most children like attention and can't differentiate between bad attention and good attention. In addition, if a mother knows about the molestation and chooses to do nothing about it, the child's guilt is multiplied.

As molested children grow up, they eventually realize that their experiences were not normal or acceptable. Once the hidden secret is out, people often ask, "What did you do to cause that person to abuse you?" or "Why didn't you stop it?" The victims think they did something to cause the abuse. In their minds, they blame themselves. Like most little children, they might have done something innocent, like run around naked after taking a bath. In such cases, adults laugh and think their children are being cute; there is nothing in this innocent action that is sexual or enticing of aberrant behavior.

> **Nothing a child could *ever* do should cause an adult to afflict abuse on her or him.**

In fact, nothing a child could ever do should

cause an adult to afflict abuse on her or him. Nothing. The responsibility always lies with the adult, the perpetrator.

The spouses of victims or the parents of a child who was molested by a non-family member can also take on the blame and false responsibility for what happened to their loved ones. "If only" can be applied to many situations. Bad things happen. The fault does not belong to the parent, the spouse, or the friend.

Many women or young people who are in a submissive position in a relationship may also experience this same sense of false responsibility and guilt. Whether the abuse is sexual, physical, or emotional, the victim blames herself or himself with comments such as, "I don't deserve anything better. I did something to cause this. It is my fault." If a rape case goes to trial, the victim is often blamed for the seduction. Often, the victims are too ashamed to admit something happened, and the criminal perpetrator goes away, only to repeat his behavior again and again.

Unfortunately, today's society is also plagued by the "date rape" drug. In such cases, the victim is helpless to fight or escape. The term "fallen woman" is pasted on the woman while the perpetrator freely goes on his way. The victim trusted the wrong person, and afterward, she carries the burden of false guilt.

In chapter nine, we discussed the topic of forgiveness. Abuse victims have to forgive the people who molested them; often, however, they also have to forgive the people who knew about the abuse and didn't do anything to protect them. For example, a mother may know that her child is being molested by the father, but she denies that it is happening. Living in fear of her husband, she can't face the possible consequences of exposing the secret. In reality, the child is not the only victim carrying the guilt; the mother carries it, too.

No matter the nature of the abuse or molestation, ministering to the victim is the same. I repeatedly ask victims, "What did you do to cause this abuse, this molestation?" They get looks of confusion or concern on their faces, not understanding why I'm asking them the same question over and over again. Suddenly, they realize that they did nothing to cause their horrible experiences. They were not at fault! They have believed a lie! If you are an abuse victim, ask yourself, *Did I cause it, or have I been believing a lie?*

After this, I ask abuse victims to say, "I have been believing a lie." If you, the reader, have experienced this situation, repeat that statement at least ten times! Repeat it ten more times if you aren't free yet. Repeat it one hundred times if you have guilt in any situation from your past. In other words, repeat that statement to yourself time and again until you know that you know that you know that you were not the cause. Release the guilt.

Young girls and women are not the only victims of abuse. Both men and women are susceptible to this problem. Divorced men and women can blame themselves for the destruction of their marriages when the blame may lie with their wayward spouses. Battered wives and husbands typically blame themselves for causing their spouses to beat them and inflict serious injuries. If this has been your experience, say this prayer right now:

> Father, what _____ did to me was sin, and it hurt me a lot. It stole my innocence from me. Take this sin from _____ and put it on the altar, never to be held against _____ again, in Jesus' name. I also lay the false responsibility and guilt that I have carried on Your altar. I know that what _____ did was wrong, and it will always be wrong. But I release _____ and hold nothing against _____. Amen.

If the abuse you suffered included any form of intercourse, you also must break an ungodly covenant.

> Father, I went into an ungodly covenant with _____. I renounce that covenant, in Jesus' name. Father, I thank You for freeing me from this ungodly covenant and from every area of false responsibility, in Jesus' name. Amen.

I've Been Believing a Lie!

Consistently listening to or being subjected to the negative can have a powerful effect on anyone. For true healing to occur, the victim has to hear positive reinforcement. There is no better way to gain self-confidence than to hear the Word of God say, "You are the apple of My eye. I love you with an everlasting love. My Son died for you. He took all your pain on the cross so you can be healed and whole! Let Me love you. Let Me be your Father. I love you so much."

When my mom was first getting acquainted with Charles, who later became my dad, I would run to answer the phone and say, "Hello, this is Dumb-Dumb!" Everyone called me "Dumb-Dumb." For many years, that was my nickname. A teacher had told my mother that I was the dumbest child she had ever encountered. I took on a label that was not true.

Charles got very upset with me when I answered his phone calls in that manner. He told me in no uncertain terms that I was never, *ever* to say those words again. He said, "You are Smart-Smart!" He still calls me "Smart-Smart" occasionally.

When someone compliments you, your response should always be, "Thank you." But when you are subjected to a constant string of negative comments that are bringing you down, do not accept the words. Back in those days, people said to me, "You are so stupid!" and my reply was, "I know!" I believed a lie. It was drilled into me every time someone told me I was dumb or stupid. Those words followed me around for many years. I lived "down" to those words until God opened my eyes.

Many times, when spouses are unfaithful, their partners blame themselves for the others' unfaithfulness. You may have been told numerous times, "His unfaithfulness is your fault. You made him turn to others."

If someone has said this to you, remember that you are not the cause. The seeds of infidelity were there long before you ever met your spouse.

False accusations can cause guilt until you realize that you are not responsible for another's choices or actions. The divorce was not my fault. My husband's unfaithfulness was not my fault. You need to shake off the words that tell you otherwise. You need to release the guilt that holds you in bondage. Please note that this applies to either spouse—the wife or the husband can be unfaithful.

> **False accusations can cause guilt until you realize that you are not responsible for another's choices or actions.**

You Are Not Responsible

Unless you encouraged your children to get involved with drugs, alcohol, promiscuity, crime, homosexuality, and so forth, you are not responsible for their actions. Progeny from very good Christian families can and do follow the path to destruction. In chapter ten, we discussed the age of accountability. Parents are responsible for their children when those children are young. Once a child reaches the age of accountability, the child has to accept responsibility for his or her own actions. As difficult as it might be, parents have to release their children to suffer the consequences for those actions.

Once children reach the age of accountability, parents must give them to God and leave them there. Parents, you can pray for your children. You should pray for them. But the ultimate responsibility for their actions lies with them. You have to trust God to do the right thing for your family, your children, your spouse, and your loved ones. He will guide and take care of them.

Maybe your children have to go through battles of their own in order to be brought to their knees before their heavenly Father to beg for forgiveness and help. That scenario often changes lives for the better. Which do you want: a child who lives a peaceful life with no problems or challenges but who ends up lost when he dies, or a child who is allowed to hit rock bottom with a physical or mental challenge that causes her to search for and accept eternal life with God?

I often ask other people to help me pray during healing services. I am giving them permission to assist in ministering to others. I may verbalize that request several times and get a response from only two or three people from the congregation. At such times, I could easily get upset and believe that I have done a poor job of teaching. Or, I can be totally obedient to God, teach what He tells me to, and leave the results up to Him. I choose to be obedient. God does the rest. No pastor or evangelist can make anyone respond to the message or make anyone do what the Bible says to do.

We are responsible for our own actions. That's enough for us to carry. Do not accept false responsibility for the actions of another. Refuse those lies. God may bring to your remembrance many situations that fit into this category. You may have to pray the prayer at the end of this section many times before you are totally free. Pray it as often as necessary to break the bondage of false responsibility, guilt, or self-blame. Those things are lies that can steal, kill, and destroy. They are lies from the enemy.

Refuse to listen to thoughts like, *If only I had done this better. If only I had done that.* You did the best that you knew how to do at the time. If you willfully did something wrong in the past, repent of that sin and God will forgive you.

When I was raising my children, I did the best I knew to do. Unfortunately, I didn't know who I was at the time; today, I could do a much better job of raising my girls. But once I discovered who God wanted me to be, I became a great mother and grandmother. I met with each of my girls and asked her forgiveness for the things I should have done differently. Everyone forgave everyone else, and God's love was victorious over the destruction that the enemy had attempted to wreak in my family.

When you become secure in who you are and what God has called you to do, you don't have to worry about all the other distractions that come at you. You will reject false responsibility. You will refuse to take on any guilt from anyone else. You will not take on other people's burdens.

Stand up and stand tall. You are a child of the King. Listen to His voice alone. Walk in His light and His might. Grow in His Word. Be healed and whole. Repeat the following prayer as often as necessary for you to get and stay completely free.

Father, I have taken false responsibility for [situation]. I have carried the guilt and the weight of this situation for a long time. Father, I take all this responsibility, all this guilt, and lay it all on Your altar, at the foot of the cross, in Jesus' name. I release the guilt, in Jesus' name. Father, take this grief from me. For any ill effects that this has had on my body, I thank You now for my healing, in Jesus' name. Amen.

When you become secure in who you are and what God has called you to do, you don't have to worry about all the other distractions that come at you.

More Testimonies

A friend of mine, Kathleen, shared the following story, which I will let her relate in her own words.

"I want to share with you my journey from a traumatic childhood to a triumphant adulthood. I say 'traumatic' because my confusion began at an early age and influenced my life for years. I never experienced a normal, carefree childhood because those whom I trusted the most stole it from me.

"By the age of eleven, my grandfather, father, and brother had all molested me. This was the beginning of my false responsibility and fearful existence. I can remember asking God never to allow my brother to touch me like that again. The next day, he died in a swimming accident.

"Even when I was a young girl, the enemy was bombarding me with many negative experiences and emotions. I was already ashamed. I felt dirty and full of fear. After my brother's death, I was filled with guilt. I falsely believed that my prayer was the reason for my brother's death.

"At the age of eleven, I believed that I was the cause of my family's pain and suffering. It was because of me that my mom and dad fell apart at the seams from losing their firstborn and only son. My two older sisters were devastated by the sudden loss of their brother. How could I tell my family that I was the reason their son and brother was gone?

"I felt alone and frightened. I decided to tell no one and keep it to myself. I could not even pray to God anymore. The enemy's plan to push me away from God was working, because I was afraid of God. I did not understand that God would never have answered a prayer by killing someone. I had not yet been exposed to John 10:10, which states, '*The thief does not come except to steal, and to kill, and to destroy. I have come that they may have life, and that they may have it more abundantly.*'

"It was sometime after my brother's death that my father molested me. I remember that day. My dad and I were at my grandparents' farm. He called me into one of the old smokehouses. I can remember as clearly as if had been yesterday: a voice inside me said, 'Do not go in there.' I did not understand what it was or where it came from, but I do remember how uneasy I felt going into that building. *If only I had listened to that voice!*

"After it happened, I said to myself, *If only I had listened to that voice.... If only I had not gone in.... What's the worst he would have done beside spanking me? Now look what you let happen to you.* I took full responsibility for my dad molesting me. In one moment, I went from a little girl who hung on every word her father had to say to one who feared his very presence. Never again would I be in the same room with him without wondering and being on guard.

"Through those younger years, I still attended and enjoyed church. Nevertheless, as I became older, I began to focus on the faults of others. I walked away from church and God. I was through with God and His people, but God was not through with me. Philippians 1:6 states that we can be '*confident of this very thing, that He who has begun a good work in you will complete it until the day of Jesus Christ.'* Looking back, I thank God that He never walked away from me.

"As I continued my day-to-day existence, I had no one in whom I could confide; therefore, I tried to bury my negative feelings. I did not know that false responsibility can open you up to many other destructive emotions, such as low self-esteem, anger, confusion, hurt, and a lack of self-worth. I became very stubborn, isolated myself from others, and had major issues with male authority.

"I remember my dad saying one day that men did not like large women. That became my safety net, and I started gaining weight to ensure that no man would look at me. I thought all those emotions were normal because I did not know what was normal. False responsibility put me on a path to self-destruction. At age thirteen, I turned to an alternative lifestyle that lasted for over twenty-five years. I went everywhere looking for acceptance from anyone who was willing to give it. I was just looking in all the wrong places.

"In 1996, I returned to God, and He lovingly began to undo all the wrong things that had happened in my life. Through His love, grace, and mercy, He delivered me from living that alternative lifestyle. Then, He gently opened my eyes.

"He showed me that there was nothing an eleven-year-old girl could have done that would cause men to molest her. God showed me that it was not my fault these men had hurt me. He showed me how I could forgive them and love them again. Yes, God performed such a miracle in my life that I had a loving relationship with my father until the day he died.

"God also showed me not so long ago that I was still hiding behind my weight. You see, God reminded me what my dad had said about men not liking large women. So, as long as I maintained my weight, I felt safe from them. I am thankful to God that He revealed this to me. I now understand why all the weight loss programs did not work. Now that my eyes have been opened by God, I can successfully lose the excess weight.

I do not have to hide anymore. I stand today completely healed and set free."

* * *

Another friend of mine has been fighting "the battle of the bulge" for many years. During this teaching, she suddenly remembered what had instigated her weight gain. When she first met her husband, she was thin and considered very attractive. She received frequent attention from men because of her appearance and demeanor. Her husband would get very upset, blaming her for the attentions of other men during her normal workday conversations and relationships, even though she never invited any inappropriate behavior.

He also called her "Gorda," telling her that it was a term of affection in Spanish. She soon learned that it meant "fatso." Thinking he wanted her to gain weight and knowing men weren't attracted to larger women, she gained weight...and more weight...and more weight. Long after her husband's death, she was still fighting the effects of his oppressive comments. She had become afraid of developing any relationships because she didn't want to be hurt again.

Today, she is free and losing weight, and she has a whole new outlook on life.

* * *

I ministered to a lady who was married to a man who loved her deeply, but she was very angry and unhappy. She had lost her joy and felt that she was of no value to her husband. She was always doing things for others, sacrificing her own happiness for everybody else and operating under the deception that everyone else's needs and desires were more important that hers.

She talked about a time early in her marriage when she had felt happy and content. The story was very different for her mother and all of her siblings, who each went through difficult times and struggles. They all had come to her with their problems, expecting her to solve them.

134

Eventually, she began to ask herself, *Why should I be so happy when they are so miserable? I don't deserve to be so happy.*

From then on, everyone else's needs became more important to her than her own, and she lost her joy. Throughout the following years, her husband would often ask, "Why can't you be happy and enjoy life?"

As she continued to talk about this situation, she remembered that during her parents' divorce, her father had come to her and told her that she would have to take care of her brothers and sister. He had said, "You're the mother now. You also need to take of your mother. She's not strong." *Why then*, she wondered, *should I have a wonderful life?* Her family was her responsibility, and she would be letting them down if she was happy and they were not.

I reached for an object from a table and handed it to her. I stepped back and didn't say anything for a minute. She stood there looking at me, and I asked her why she had taken it. We laughed, but she caught the revelation. It was up to her how long she held onto it. She had to choose to set it down and release the responsibility.

I asked her repeatedly if she was responsible for the happiness of her brothers and sister. She finally exclaimed, "No!" Of course, she cared for them and desired for them to be happy, but she understood that she was not responsible for the choices they had made.

My next question surprised her. "Is your husband responsible for your happiness?"

She softly responded, "No."

If someone approaches you and hands you a large box, you will probably take it, right? If the giver walks away, you must hold it or carry it—unless you decide to put it down. There is an implied acceptance of responsibility for the item when you receive it. You can accept it or not. In this example, we are speaking of a tangible item, but packages of responsibility are handed to us daily in many shapes and sizes!

We are responsible to others—to help them, encourage them, and love them (see Galatians 6:1–2)—but we are *not* responsible for the choices others make. There is a big difference.

* * *

I have a friend whose father was an alcoholic. She recalled an incident when her father was drunk, and she would not go near him. He asked, "Don't you love your daddy?" and she simply replied, "You're not my daddy!"

Thirteen years later, on the night before her wedding, he told her that her statement was so powerful that he had quit drinking. She had never thought about the years that her father stayed sober.

As the years passed, her own husband's drinking became more and more of a problem, and she began to doubt her worth and his love for her. After all, her father had stopped drinking because of her.

She began to take on the responsibility for her husband's problem. As long as she took the responsibility for her husband's drinking, he didn't have to! Eventually, she realized that she had been believing a lie. She had no control over his choices. Her husband was left to face the responsibility for his own choices. She no longer carried them—even when he tried to hand them to her.

> **If you pick up the responsibility for people's failure to be healed, then who holds the responsibility if they do get healed?**

I have seen a similar mind-set in people I have prayed for—even members of my ministry team who have struggled with the deaths of people they prayed for or with situations where they did not see immediate manifestations of healing and freedom. One person asked me what he was doing wrong. I answered him with a question: "Whose responsibility is it to heal them?"

If you pick up the responsibility for people's failure to be healed, then who holds the responsibility if they do get healed? If we begin to think that there is something we must do to get them healed, then we are picking up Jesus' responsibility. *He* has given us the authority to use *His* name.

The Responsibility Is His

Have you done something that you wished you hadn't done? Have you carried the guilt of your actions through the years?

Many times, I have ministered to those who have had an affair inside or outside of marriage. The guilt for their inappropriate actions has crippled them. I don't need to tell these people that they shouldn't have done what they did, because they have been browbeating themselves ever since it happened. It is time to get free from *all* guilt.

Recently, I was ministering to a friend who had made a poor decision many years earlier. I told her that she would survive as long a she did not continue to beat herself up over it. She had to give it to God and allow His healing to restore her.

Even though we ask for and receive God's forgiveness for our sins, we often still let the sins weigh heavily on our hearts and minds. The guilt is too much for us to bear. We must be willing to release it all to God and allow His healing and forgiveness to wipe all the guilt away. Pray this prayer to release yourself from guilt:

> Father, what I did was wrong, and it was sin. I repent of this sin and ask You to take it from me and put it on the cross, never to be held against me again. I have carried this guilt for what I did, and I don't want to carry it anymore. I lay it on Your altar; I give it up freely. Show me how to accept Your forgiveness. Father, I ask that You bless _____ [anyone you may have hurt], in Jesus' name. Amen.

CHAPTER 11
Salvation

Life encompasses dangers and unpleasant things as well as fun events and blessings. When we face the negative, we search our minds for a way out. We do not have the ultimate answer, but God does. It would be so much easier to go directly to Him when we need answers instead of trying to figure out our problems on our own, but pride, self-reliance, and independence rear their ugly heads, and we often endeavor to fight the battles alone.

Salvation in the Old Testament

In the garden, Adam and Eve had the counsel of the Almighty, which they chose to reject. They were then separated from close communion with Him. For years, man didn't enjoy intimacy with his Creator.

Obviously, a few righteous men throughout the Old Testament had faith in God. They knew that God would take care of them and protect them from evil and destruction. They knew God was their ultimate salvation. These chosen few enjoyed God's peace, His communion, and His voice. They obeyed that voice and attempted to share His words with others, even when the world around them didn't welcome or listen very well. Most people of that day went their own selfish ways. Even miracles, signs, and wonders didn't have long-lasting effects on most of them.

In the Christian religion, salvation commonly means deliverance from sin, or from the consequences of sin, through Jesus Christ's death on the cross. It also designates somebody or something that protects or delivers another from harm, destruction, difficulty, or failure.

However, salvation goes back thousands of years before Christ was born. In fact, the King James Version of the Bible first uses the term in Genesis 49:18, and *salvation* is mentioned throughout the entire Old

Testament. Many of those same verses have been used as the basis for some of our favorite praise songs through the years.

Let's examine the words of Moses, David, Isaiah, and other prophets.

The LORD is my strength and song, and He has become my salvation; He is my God, and I will praise Him; my father's God, and I will exalt Him. (Exodus 15:2)

I have trusted in Your mercy; my heart shall rejoice in Your salvation. (Psalm 13:5)

You have also given me the shield of Your salvation; Your right hand has held me up, Your gentleness has made me great. (Psalm 18:35)

The LORD lives! Blessed be my Rock! Let the God of my salvation be exalted. (Psalm 18:46)

The LORD is my light and my salvation; whom shall I fear? The Lord is the strength of my life; of whom shall I be afraid? (Psalm 27:1)

The salvation of the righteous is from the LORD; He is their strength in the time of trouble. (Psalm 37:39)

Restore to me the joy of Your salvation, and uphold me by Your generous Spirit. (Psalm 51:12)

Let all those who seek You rejoice and be glad in You; and let those who love Your salvation say continually, "Let God be magnified!" (Psalm 70:4)

He shall call upon Me, and I will answer him; I will be with him in trouble; I will deliver him and honor him. With long life I will satisfy him, and show him My salvation. (Psalm 91:15–16)

God is my salvation; I will trust, and not be afraid: for the LORD

Jehovah is my strength and my song; he also is become my salvation. (Isaiah 12:2 KJV)

Lift up your eyes to the heavens, and look on the earth beneath. For the heavens will vanish away like smoke, the earth will grow old like a garment, and those who dwell in it will die in like manner; but My salvation will be forever, and My righteousness will not be abolished. (Isaiah 51:6)

How beautiful upon the mountains are the feet of him who brings good news, who proclaims peace, who brings glad tidings of good things, who proclaims salvation, who says to Zion, "Your God reigns!" (Isaiah 52:7)

For He put on righteousness as a breastplate, and a helmet of salvation on His head; He put on the garments of vengeance for clothing, and was clad with zeal as a cloak. (Isaiah 59:17)

I will greatly rejoice in the LORD, my soul shall be joyful in my God; for He has clothed me with the garments of salvation, He has covered me with the robe of righteousness, as a bridegroom decks himself with ornaments, and as a bride adorns herself with her jewels. (Isaiah 61:10)

Yet I will rejoice in the LORD, I will joy in the God of my salvation. (Habakkuk 3:18)

It is obvious that these men of God found His peace. They experienced His joy. They understood obedience to His Word and had intimate relationships with their God. However, something was still missing.

Salvation under the New Covenant

Knowing that animal sacrifices for sin would always be insufficient, God provided humanity with the ultimate sacrifice—one that would wipe out sin forever for those who believed. He sent His Son.

For God so loved the world that He gave His only begotten Son, that whoever believes in Him should not perish but have everlasting life.
(John 3:16)

Once and for all time, God's Son willingly gave up His life upon the cross so everyone born from that day forward could be saved from eternal damnation—total separation from God. Instead of killing animals and dealing with burnt and bloody sacrifices, people simply had to believe in Jesus and His ultimate sacrifice for everyone.

Were people in Jesus' time so bad that they wouldn't believe it could be so simple? Did they think God couldn't change the rules—His command to sacrifice living things? Were the religious leaders afraid of God's wrath or of losing control of the people, who were probably more afraid of the temple priests than they were of God?

The scales that blinded them from the truth condemned them to destruction—not the destruction of life, but the destruction leading to total and eternal separation from God after their earthly bodies ceased to exist.

But those who believed found His ultimate love, His peace, and His joy. The cares of the world fell away as His love replaced the daily aches and pains of worldly life. The simple request for forgiveness for their sins was all they needed. *"Ask, and you will receive"* (John 16:24). They believed in Him and in His words. Joy filled their hearts. Peace invaded their minds. Heaven was assured when they received Him.

To give knowledge of salvation to His people by the remission of their sins.... (Luke 1:77)

Nor is there salvation in any other, for there is no other name under heaven given among men by which we must be saved. (Acts 4:12)

For I am not ashamed of the gospel of Christ, for it is the power of God to salvation for everyone who believes, for the Jew first and also for the Greek. (Romans 1:16)

For with the heart one believes unto righteousness, and with the mouth confession is made unto salvation. (Romans 10:10)

Every tongue should confess that Jesus Christ is Lord, to the glory of God the Father. Therefore, my beloved, as you have always obeyed, not as in my presence only, but now much more in my absence, work out your own salvation with fear and trembling; for it is God who works in you both to will and to do for His good pleasure. (Philippians 2:11–13)

Let us who are of the day be sober, putting on the breastplate of faith and love, and as a helmet the hope of salvation. For God did not appoint us to wrath, but to obtain salvation through our Lord Jesus Christ, who died for us, that whether we wake or sleep, we should live together with Him. (1 Thessalonians 5:8–10)

We are bound to give thanks to God always for you, brethren beloved by the Lord, because God from the beginning chose you for salvation through sanctification by the Spirit and belief in the truth. (2 Thessalonians 2:13)

From childhood you have known the Holy Scriptures, which are able to make you wise for salvation through faith which is in Christ Jesus. (2 Timothy 3:15)

For the grace of God that brings salvation has appeared to all men. (Titus 2:11)

Are they not all ministering spirits sent forth to minister for those who will inherit salvation? (Hebrews 1:14)

How shall we escape if we neglect so great a salvation, which at the first began to be spoken by the Lord, and was confirmed to us by those who heard Him…? (Hebrews 2:3)

Though He was a Son, yet He learned obedience by the things which He suffered. And having been perfected, He became the author of eternal salvation to all who obey Him, called by God as High Priest "according to the order of Melchizedek." (Hebrews 5:8–10)

As it is appointed for men to die once, but after this the judgment, so Christ was offered once to bear the sins of many. To those who eagerly wait for Him He will appear a second time, apart from sin, for salvation. (Hebrews 9:27–28)

The Ultimate Sacrifice for the Sins of All Men

Logical minds have a hard time understanding the true implications and power of Jesus' sacrifice. But those of us who have experienced Him can never deny His power or love. His followers didn't understand why He had to die, but He did. As a man on the earth, He could minister only to a few at a time. After His death—His sacrifice—He could send His Holy Spirit to live within any and every person on earth who believed in Him. His power, love, joy, and peace could then spread exponentially across the earth.

God planted a seed—His Son. He then reaped a marvelous harvest—thousands and thousands of believers throughout the ages. Think of it! He saved all of us. All we have to do is believe. We don't have to work for it or meet some quota of good deeds to earn our salvation. We just have to believe in Jesus.

What does He save us from? Ultimate death and destruction; an afterlife in the pits of hell. Many have heard the preachers who spout "hellfire and damnation" in order to scare people into heaven. Some people may need that. But there is so much more. Some people confess their sins and slide into heaven at the last minute. Praise God, they are going to heaven; however, there is so much more than that.

God so loved the world and His creation that He provided a way for every one of His creatures to be reconciled back to Him. No longer is there a separation. Intimacy is possible. He can walk with us again,

We can have God's help and protection today, right here, right now.

talk with us again. He can truly be our best Friend while we are living on this earth. We don't have to wait until we get to heaven to enjoy His peace, love, and joy. We can have His help and protection today, right here, right now.

Don't Lose Your Salvation

How can we be assured of His constant help and protection? Remember what we have learned. Sin separates us from God. Repentance brings us back. Obedience keeps us there under His protection. Picture a large umbrella. I like to think of it as the protection of His wings spoken of in the Old Testament. (See, for example, Psalm 91:4.) He is our hiding place. He protects us from the enemy. He takes care of us and surrounds us with songs.

He shall cover you with His feathers, and under His wings you shall take refuge; His truth shall be your shield and buckler.

(Psalm 91:4)

You are my hiding place; You shall preserve me from trouble; You shall surround me with songs of deliverance. (Psalm 32:7)

You are my refuge and my shield; your word is my source of hope.

(Psalm 119:114 NLT)

Under His wings, His umbrella, believers are hidden away from the enemy. Obedience to His Word keeps the believer under that umbrella. Sin or disobedience causes the person to step out from under that umbrella of protection. It opens the door for the enemy to enter and attack. Repentance brings the person quickly back under God's protection again.

Remember: God never walks away from us. We are the ones who create the chasm of separation. If you don't feel or haven't felt God's presence

144

lately, ask Him what has happened. If you can't think of a specific reason, repent anyway. Seek His face and regain that presence.

When people get saved and turn their lives over to Christ, many also get miraculously healed. This is scriptural, too, even though it does not happen in every case.

> *But to you who fear My name the Sun of Righteousness shall arise with healing in His wings; and you shall go out and grow fat like stall-fed calves.* (Malachi 4:2)

How can some people profess to be believers and yet act like the lost of the world? Many take God for granted. They know that He will forgive them when they ask, so they purposefully sin. They have affairs, they use God's name in vain, they abuse their spouses or children, and they get involved with cultic practices on Saturday nights before going to church on Sunday.

Many truly believe that their "hidden" sins are nothing to worry about. Sorry, God sees and knows about them all. No one can hide from Him. He wants our total repentance from everything not of Him. He doesn't want us to alter our present path by just an inch or two. He wants a complete turnaround. He isn't asking for our obedience once in a while. He wants it each and every day.

Salvation Must Be Real

In modern cultures, most people have heard of Jesus. Indeed, many believe that He is the Son of God, was born in a manger, and died on a cross. They may have even said the sinner's prayer at one time in their lives. But they have not changed. They have not allowed God to have control of their lives. They have not welcomed Jesus Christ into their hearts. They certainly don't understand or listen to the Holy Spirit.

If asked, "Do you believe in Jesus?" these people may respond with something like, "Yes, I know who He was."

Personally, I don't particularly like the question, "Are you saved?" Many will reply with, "Saved from what?"

I would rather ask, "Do you know Jesus as your personal confidant and best friend? Does He go with you everywhere you go and guide every action you take with love and peace? Has He changed your life?"

When people have truly given their lives to Jesus, there are obvious outward signs. Instead of short tempers, they exude peace. Instead of crass, ugly words, they respond to problems with calm, thoughtful replies. Instead of fixed, stressed appearances, they are relaxed.

With God, we no longer have to rely simply on our own resources or our own independent choices.

Without God, we can rely only on our previous experiences to deal with the crises of today. I am not discounting intelligence, experience, or common sense at all. With God, however, we no longer have to rely simply on our own resources or our own independent choices. A Christian's usual response should be, "Father, I need Your advice in this situation. Jesus, You are living in me. I need Your help here. Holy Spirit, give me the words to speak. Tell me what to do."

The crisis of the day may indeed respond to your learned solution. Great. However, if you need an answer, ask the One who has all the answers. If the cause of the problem is a spiritual battle, you really need His guidance first, not last. So, ask.

While doing the research for this book, I came across the following version of 1 Peter. I could choose to continue on explaining the positive aspects of salvation to you. However, I am going to let you read Peter's account from *The Message* Bible instead. Here's the first chapter from 1 Peter. It really does say it all.

What a God we have! And how fortunate we are to have him, this Father of our Master Jesus! Because Jesus was raised from the dead, we've been given a brand-new life and have everything to live for, including a future in heaven—and the future starts now! God is keeping careful watch over us and the future. The Day is coming when you'll have it all—life healed and whole.

I know how great this makes you feel, even though you have to put up with every kind of aggravation in the meantime. Pure gold put in the fire comes out of it proved pure; genuine faith put through this suffering comes out proved genuine. When Jesus wraps this all up, it's your faith, not your gold, that God will have on display as evidence of his victory.

You never saw him, yet you love him. You still don't see him, yet you trust him—with laughter and singing. Because you kept on believing, you'll get what you're looking forward to: total salvation.

The prophets who told us this was coming asked a lot of questions about this gift of life God was preparing. The Messiah's Spirit let them in on some of it—that the Messiah would experience suffering, followed by glory. They clamored to know who and when. All they were told was that they were serving you, you who by orders from heaven have now heard for yourselves—through the Holy Spirit— the Message of those prophecies fulfilled. Do you realize how fortunate you are? Angels would have given anything to be in on this!

So roll up your sleeves, put your mind in gear, be totally ready to receive the gift that's coming when Jesus arrives. Don't lazily slip back into those old grooves of evil, doing just what you feel like doing. You didn't know any better then; you do now. As obedient children, let yourselves be pulled into a way of life shaped by God's life, a life energetic and blazing with holiness. God said, "I am holy; you be holy."

You call out to God for help and he helps—he's a good Father that way. But don't forget, he's also a responsible Father, and won't let you get by with sloppy living.

Your life is a journey you must travel with a deep consciousness of God. It cost God plenty to get you out of that dead-end, empty-headed life you grew up in. He paid with Christ's sacred blood, you know. He died like an unblemished, sacrificial lamb. And this was no afterthought. Even though it has only lately—at the end of the ages—become public knowledge, God always knew he was going to do this for you. It's because of this sacrificed Messiah, whom God then raised from the dead and glorified, that you trust God, that you know you have a future in God.

Now that you've cleaned up your lives by following the truth, love one another as if your lives depended on it. Your new life is not like your old life. Your old birth came from mortal sperm; your new birth comes from God's living Word. Just think: a life conceived by God himself!   (1 Peter 1:3–23)

Are you ready for a new life? A new birth? Once you accept God as your Father, your family changes. Your genealogy changes. You are now a member of His family. You can still remember the things you experienced in the past, but it feels like those things happened to another person. The decisions of yesteryear may seem strange to you in the light of the new revelation you feel now. Even reading the Bible will be different. You may have read the same verse for years, and suddenly, you understand its meaning from a totally new perspective. It is a marvelous feeling.

> **To be effective in this world, to be used of God, you do need a total, sold-out commitment to Him.**

Maybe you just need to recommit your life to God with a new and better understanding of what life in Christ really entails. To be effective in this world, to be used of God, you do need a total, sold-out commitment to Him.

Open up your heart right now. Listen to Him. Follow His leading, not just my words. Man can fail you. God can't and won't ever fail you. He keeps His promises. He loves you so much. You are His special child, and He wants you to curl up in His arms and feel His eternal, everlasting, unconditional love.

Father, I want to ask Your forgiveness right now, today. I need You in my life. I have depended on my own experiences and conditioned responses to life's crises and problems instead of listening to You. At times, I have willfully and knowingly done things against Your Word and Your commandments. I have not followed Your guidance. I have gone my own way so many times. I ask for Your forgiveness right now. Separate my sins from me and put them on the cross. I break all curses that have been spoken against me. I receive all Your blessings and give You all the praise and glory.

Jesus, live within me forever. I give You complete control of my heart. I believe in You, the one and only Son of God. You gave Your life for me so I could have eternal life in heaven, totally reconciled to my Father. Thank You, Jesus.

Father, I dedicate and commit my life to You. I will do my best to follow Your Word every day of my life with my thoughts, my words, and my actions. I want to be used by You. I want to be a vessel of honor, reaching out to others who are hurting and in need of Your salvation and healing power. I want to tell the whole world what You have done for me. Thank You, in Jesus' name. Amen.

CHAPTER 12

The Baptism of the Holy Spirit

I want it all!

Sometimes a controversial subject within mainstream churches, the baptism in the Holy Spirit is one of the hallmarks of the Spirit-filled life. Thankfully, many in mainstream churches are finding and enjoying the power of the Holy Spirit today like never before. They are remaining in their denominations but enjoying the ultimate power of God.

What is it? Where do you get it? What does it do? What do you have to do to receive it? It sounds complicated, but it is as simple as getting saved.

You heard the salvation message, you believed, you asked Jesus to come into your heart, and you received. The baptism in the Holy Spirit can occur the same way. Some actually have received without asking, but everyone receives by faith.

When you ask Jesus to come into your life, you open up your heart for Him to change you into a new person with a new way of thinking and acting. You actually receive a new way of living. Understanding this simple truth can be difficult for some, but it doesn't take more than simple faith the size of a mustard seed.

Do you trust God to take care of you and those you love? Do you believe that you are going to heaven? Do you believe that Jesus lives in your heart? Then, believe and trust Him for His Holy Spirit, also. Many teachers say we

I want it all!

receive His Spirit when we are saved. Indeed, this is true. We do receive Jesus and His Holy Spirit when we are saved. However, we also have to allow Him to work in our lives. We have to make that choice.

150

Many Spirit-filled saints believe that a person has to "speak in tongues" as evidence that he has truly received the Holy Spirit through the baptism. Through my travels, I have encountered multitudes of people at various stages in their spiritual journeys. You probably have, too. I've met everyone from the not saved, once saved, newly saved, totally saved, Spirit-led, Spirit-filled, to totally sold-out and Spirit-directed in all areas of life.

Many within the five-fold ministry ranks and congregations are indeed Spirit-led. They are led by the Spirit of God, and they seek His face with all sincerity and devotion. However, they may not speak in tongues. Many lack the Spirit-power that comes with the baptism of the Holy Spirit, as well as the fruit and gifts of the Spirit.

An outward, obvious evidence of the Holy Spirit baptism is "speaking in tongues" or praying in a language other than one you have learned or studied. Speaking in tongues means overcoming one of the last barriers to total obedience to God.

Overcoming Barriers to Trust

In general, we don't want anyone telling us what to say or think. We are our "own person" and can speak what we choose, when we choose, and how we choose. Part of living, however, is learning how to exercise control. Sometimes, we call it "tact" and use it so we don't insult people; those with no control are called "rude" or "uncouth." We learn to use proper language for the occasion and not to use vulgar, inappropriate comments or words. We learn when, what, where, and how to say certain things.

These rules are very important to us; however, these rules can also block some people from speaking in tongues with the Holy Spirit baptism. Relinquishing control of one's mouth can be difficult and, for some, nearly impossible.

> **Release control to God; allow Him to speak through you, bypassing your thoughts and understanding.**

Giving God ultimate trust in all areas of life

151

includes surrendering control of our "unruly" member—the tongue. Release control to God; allow Him to speak through you, bypassing your thoughts and understanding. You don't need to know the language you speak or what words to say. You actually don't need to understand any part of what you are saying or praying. As the Bible says, you are speaking to Him! (See 1 Corinthians 14:27–28.) And He understands everything. He understands your heart, no matter what words are uttered.

Have you ever wanted to pray for a specific need, whether personal or for someone else, but you couldn't find the words to speak? We all have had that problem many, many times. By allowing God to speak through us, we are praying to our Father with perfect, appropriate words. To pray properly with our minds, we need the nitty-gritty details of the situation and knowledge of all aspects of the problem. But with the Holy Spirit in control, we don't need any details. In fact, at times, God will simply bring a face or name to mind with the impression that prayer is needed... *immediately!* By praying in the Spirit, or in tongues, the Holy Spirit gives your spirit the perfect words to pray for that particular situation.

He may awaken you in the middle of the night with a need to pray for someone on the other side of the world. While you pray, you may feel an aching heart; you may cry tears of sorrow. However, after a time, you will experience the utter joy and peace of knowing that the situation is being handled by the King of kings and Lord of lords.

I often wonder how many saints around the world have been called to arms—called to their knees—during those midnight hours to pray in obedience to His prompting. As part of His army here on earth, we don't carry weapons created by man. We do, however, carry the most powerful weapon available in the universe—His Holy Spirit and the perfect way to pray.

The power of words is underrated in today's world. Our words activate God's angels. Backed up with His Spirit, our words can send the devils of hell back where they belong. His protection can be sent across the planet by a simple prayer in words we don't understand. How marvelous is our God! He truly has provided everything we need. We just have to learn, believe, receive, and trust in His solutions to our problems instead of our own inept attempts to save ourselves and handle the challenges of life.

Yes, He has given us minds to use, common sense to apply, and many life lessons to learn. But knowing when to apply what we have learned still takes guidance and direction. Usually, we try to do everything according to man's instructions, but sometimes, we need that extra bit of wisdom to simplify the steps to ultimate success.

Where do you go to receive His Spirit? Where are you now? Yes, many have received the Spirit at church or at a gathering of believers. But there is no restriction or perfect environment. Wherever you are is fine. And now is always a good time. Testimonies of those who received His Spirit can be quite amazing, as well as very amusing. God will make every experience unique and unforgettable.

Receiving the Baptism

One person started speaking in tongues while driving down the road in his car. Another received it in the middle of her bubble bath. Another was awakened in the middle of the night by her own voice speaking in tongues.

Whether one at a time or as part of a group standing at the altar, people seeking and truly wanting God's Spirit will receive Him. God is just waiting for willing hearts. Thousands of people around the world have received His Spirit under the instruction of my dad, Charles Hunter, at the ends of the services he held with my mom for many years of ministry.

> **People seeking and truly wanting God's Spirit will receive Him. God is just waiting for willing hearts.**

My mom and dad received the baptism in 1972. They had been searching it out, and some of the experiences in their book are hysterical. Looking at it from a natural mind and trying to imitate it, describe it, or even understand it is impossible.

My parents finally received the baptism and

wanted me to get it, also. They would have meetings and tell the guest speaker that I had not yet received the baptism. One speaker after another would call me out in front of fifty to a thousand people. Each would try to minister this marvelous experience to me using the microphone so everyone could hear. I was timid and had low self-esteem, so each event was nothing but traumatizing to me.

I went to Oral Roberts University for my first year of college. A girl in my dorm prayed in tongues and sang in tongues *so loudly* that it amazed me. Then, she would cuss. Based on previous teachings at my church, I didn't believe that what she was doing was of God. It was of the devil; it made her cuss! I had never cussed, and I certainly didn't want to start.

My parents were determined to make sure I got the baptism of the Spirit. You can imagine what I felt in my heart. All I wanted was *all* of God! After my first year at Oral Roberts University and all the other things that had happened, I cried out to God, "If this is of You, *I want it all!*"

On May 16, 1973, in the privacy of my dad's study (company was staying in my bedroom), I was baptized with the Holy Spirit. In a small voice, I began to speak in tongues. It was nothing major; it was very quiet. I didn't tell anyone for quite a while. And you know what? It didn't make me cuss! It gave me greater power to serve God and a greater anointing to hear Him and to be used of Him. However, it didn't make me instantly perfect.

Living the Spirit-Filled Life

When I first bent my knee to His total will, I wanted everything He had to offer. I saw the marvelous life change He had worked within my mother. I wanted whatever she had. Without Jesus, without God, without His Holy Spirit in my life, I would have been destroyed long ago. I can't even imagine what my life would be like without Him.

However, I do know what my life is now. I know what He has done for me. I witness daily what He does through me. I am a walking miracle, and I freely share that miracle with everyone I meet. I could choose to wallow in the sorrows and woes of the challenges life throws at me, but instead, I rebuke the negative; I refuse to accept or allow the attacks of the devil to drag me into the pit of destruction. I reject the lies the enemy whispers into my mind.

The devil always repeats the same tricks, so I know he does the same thing to you. When the negative attacks come, remember that the battle is the Lord's. What should you do? The same thing I do: pray in tongues. As the pressure rises, pray louder and faster. Better yet, sing in tongues.

When you put your trust in His direction, His Word, and His Spirit, the situation can do a complete turnaround in front of your eyes. Let a miracle happen once, and you will never forget it. I have even woken up in the middle of a bad dream speaking in tongues. God works even while you sleep.

> **Let a miracle happen once, and you will never forget it.**

We have heard and quoted the following Scripture numerous times throughout the years: *"Where two or three are gathered together in My name, I am there in the midst of them"* (Matthew 18:20). Truly, there is power when two or more believers are together and praying in agreement—even by phone or Internet. However, that power is multiplied innumerable times when the prayer warriors are Spirit-filled.

Are you a parent? I am. A grandparent? I am. Do you have an unsaved spouse? (Thank God, mine is a wonderfully saved spiritual rock for me.) Do you have other loved ones with major issues in their lives? We all do. How do we pray? How do we give them the help they need to get the victory?

I do not have magic words. I do not have all the answers. But I do know who does. And I do know how to plug into the Source of ultimate wisdom and power—the One who has all the answers to everyone's problems.

Speak in tongues. Pray in tongues. Sing in tongues. If you're in a crowd, think in tongues.

Years ago, I heard an interesting story that you can apply at any time. If we hear people talking to themselves, we immediately wonder about their sanity. Even if they speak in a different language, their mental status will be in question. However, if someone is walking down the aisle at the grocery store and singing in another language, people will be more likely to think, "What a wonderful voice. That person is so happy!" No one will know that you are singing in tongues.

For those of you who believe you can't sing or are tone-deaf, don't worry. Amazingly, many "tone-deaf" people can sing beautifully in the Spirit. Such an experience is a true miracle that no one can take away from you.

Allowing the Spirit to reign over your life has marvelous results in many areas. When you have total faith in Him, He can give you the ability to do things you have not done before. For instance, a friend of mine could play the piano quite well as long as the printed music was in front of her. In fact, she could sight-read almost anything given to her. However, she could not memorize music. Weeks of practice for recitals became torture during her teen years of music lessons. Years later, after her experience with the Holy Spirit, she allowed the Spirit to play through her hands. She now plays songs that she has never learned. She plays music she has never heard before. She can play with her eyes closed. Her music is peace to her soul and to others who listen.

Many beautiful songs of praise and worship have been created by willing vessels. Books have been written, sermons have been delivered, and prayers have been spoken without being planned or researched by the person. God is the Source.

Once you comprehend the concept of being truly led, filled, and directed by the Holy Spirit, you will never again doubt that God wrote every word of the Holy Bible through His chosen servants. He hasn't stopped speaking or working through His children. All new revelations and new insights come from Him. His miracles continue to this day. He *"is the same yesterday, today, and forever"* (Hebrews 13:8).

One of the amazing things that happens after the Holy Spirit baptism is the increased understanding of the Scriptures. The verse saying, *"there fell from his eyes something like scales"* (Acts 9:18) has a brand-new meaning. Suddenly, the Bible becomes more alive. It speaks to your heart in ways you could never have imagined before. Verses pop into your mind to fit the situation at hand more readily. Meanings of Scriptures jump into your mind—even while reading the "begats."

Your priorities in life change. Things that you thought were important before suddenly become inconsequential. For instance, the desire to make money for personal gain and pleasure suddenly becomes the need to finance the gospel and promote God's Word. Buying numerous presents for people who already have more than they need becomes a desire to feed the starving and give gifts to the children who have nothing.

The question "What Would Jesus Do?" can be answered by His Spirit—anytime and anywhere. Are you ready? Are you willing? Do you want everything God has planned for His children? Do you want to join His army and receive the weapons only He can provide?

Your age doesn't matter. Your sex doesn't matter. Where you live doesn't matter. Your health doesn't matter. A willing heart is what He wants. You may be very young or very old. You may be training for a marathon or be paralyzed and dependent on others. Your physical or mental situation doesn't stop you from receiving His power through His Holy Spirit.

Your age doesn't matter. Where you live doesn't matter. A willing heart is what He wants.

Some people believe and use the manifestations of the Holy Spirit and His anointing interchangeably. There are definite differences in all aspects of the Spirit, however, even when they are all intertwined together in a life. Yet in every circumstance, God's power is magnified to His glory in remarkable ways.

157

Are You Ready?

Repeat this prayer:

Father, I want everything You have for me. I ask You to baptize me with Your Holy Spirit, with the evidence of speaking in tongues. Thank You, Jesus! Amen.

Open your mouth and begin worshipping Him! Allow Him to flow through you, your mouth, your mind, and your body.

CHAPTER 13

Healing Is a Way of Life

After learning what to do, you have a greater responsibility than ever before. Now, when someone around you needs help or healing, you can quickly and easily reach out with answers as you allow Jesus to work through you.

Let me explain the difference between miracles and healings. Miracles are instantaneous. Healings take time. Both are the work of God's healing hand through you. Some people may claim that nothing happened when you prayed. Encourage them to believe in their total healing, because occasionally, it does take time to manifest. It is our choice whether to accept the healing or reject it.

God can use people every day and everywhere. You don't have to be part of an official ministry to lay hands on the sick and see them recover. The Great Commission was given to all believers. This means that every believer has the authority to pray for others.

> **God can use people every day and everywhere.**

I have told you many stories of healing throughout this book. Now, I want to devote this chapter to sharing with you the testimonies I have received through the last few years from everyday believers who have taken this teaching and put it to good use.

Testimonies from Everyday People Being Used by God

"Just wanted to let you all know again what a tremendous blessing it was to host Joan Hunter Ministries. The testimonies are coming in daily.

"My family, who are very traditional and spiritually behind, were totally transformed. Just when I thought they didn't really get it, they stayed up all night, walking through repentance, forgiveness, and deliverance from various situations—some older than I am! Emotional healing, which is what they need the most, has begun for Georgia! Hallelujah!

"Those who participated in the school are already stepping into the opportunities to pray for people and are excited to hear the joy of those prayed for."

—L. S.

* * *

"Before anything else, I want to bless you and bless the ministry that you have. When you visited our church in Guatemala, my mother and I visited on Wednesday. She did not believe in what was happening that night with the move of the Holy Spirit. When you said that somebody needed a new heart, she received it. She received a physically and spiritually new heart. She had been a bitter woman, but she changed into a whole new woman, full of sweetness and with a brand-new, healed heart.

"Also, when you prayed for new prostate glands for the men, I cried out for my father to receive healing, even though he was not there. He went to the doctor and was examined. He is healed and normal. He does not have anything wrong with him now. I was also healed of knee pain that had been bothering me so much.

"You prayed for a boy who needed a new brain. Afterward, he told you that he had nothing wrong with him and that he had no idea what had happened to him. I want to tell you that when you were praying for him, the Holy Spirit allowed me to see many angels coming down and covering everyone. An enormous brilliance was behind you, and I could see the silhouettes of angels. It is something I will never forget and will always be grateful to God for having allowed me to see.

"When we went to lend aid at another church, I was a witness to the healing of lungs on a woman sitting next to me. Just like the Holy Spirit allowed your translators to feel the healings, I too was blessed to feel her healing.

"God bless you, Joan, for being a precious instrument of God. May He can continue using you for healings for his people. Blessings on your calling."

—D. C.

* * *

"Joan, I know that you have touched the lives of many people, including myself, but I want you to know that when you came to our church and conducted your healing ministry with the impartation of your healing gift, I was healed. I couldn't lift anything more than a few pounds with my right arm because the rotator cuff in my right shoulder was torn.

"I am now going to the YMCA and working out on Nautilus equipment and working my way up to the heavier free weights. Thank you, and may God's love, grace, and mercy continue to shine on you, your family, and your ministry. Once again, thank you and your wonderful co-facilitators of God's healing."

—J. F.

* * *

"Thank you for the conference and workshop this weekend. Joan, your teaching was wonderful. You make it look so easy. Your instructions helped me to understand that when we minister, there are sometimes things that the Lord wants to heal or take care of in addition to the initial physical problem. During this teaching, I became very aware that the physical stuff people exhibit is sometimes a result of an inner healing that's needed.

"May we minister to the needs of His body, listening, hearing, and being bold to trust that *He is the God who still heals!* As we go forth, may He be glorified! By having these conferences, you are helping to impart all that God has to be released into His children as we go out."

—M. B.

* * *

"Joan, I wanted to share my testimony with you. I *know* God has healed the severe back pain that I've experienced for dozens of years, which was caused from multiple traumas. I believe that the degenerative disc disease, herniated discs, and fractured vertebrae throughout my entire lumbar, thoracic, and cervical spine has been healed, in Jesus' name.

"I know God has healed the severe pain in my knees and ankles, diagnosed one week before as gout. I'm so glad I didn't start the new medicine! No confusion here on what cured the pain! I know God has healed the severe pain that I have been experiencing in my left kidney for the past year as a result of decreasing renal function. I'm believing God for not only a new left kidney, but also for a new one on the right side, which was removed three years ago.

"God has healed the severe pain that I've had in my left shoulder, elbow, and hand! Multiple surgeries and therapy hadn't released this pain totally…*but God!* God has healed the severe pain that I've experienced in my neurogenic bladder for the past twenty years. I'm believing God for a brand-new bladder. I'm so excited that I declined the surgery to my bladder just six weeks ago!

"These are just a few of the things I *know* God did for me. I'm sure more revelation will be made clear to me as I slowly adjust to this new life of being pain-free. I'm just realizing now that my left foot, which has been partially amputated, isn't swollen and thumping! *Praise God!* I'll be one of 'The King's Kids,' turning in my handicap license plate!"

—L. R.

* * *

"Your book is really good for ministering to the whole man. A mentally challenged undergraduate was prayed for using the information in your book. She is totally healed now and back to the university, continuing her studies. Praise the Lord."

—V. F.

* * *

"While at the Christian Bookseller's Association, I prayed for a Baptist lady in the next booth. She was healed of arthritis. I laid my hand on her knee and 'spoke' a new knee into her, 'cursed' the arthritis, and 'commanded' it to go—and it did.

"We all had our eyes open, smiling just like we were having a conversation with each other. She turned to the lady next to her and said, 'I can't believe I got healed. I thought you had to roll all over the floor to get healed.' It was very simple and quiet, but powerful—and a done deal."

* * *

"The children's teacher called me the day after you prayed to say that she sees a marked improvement in my son. When she told my son of her observation, he announced, 'Yes! Because I have a new brain!'"

* * *

"I have been ministering to all who will listen to me to accept their healings and praise God. I feel so empowered by the Lord! I am not hesitant or unsure to speak to those who have reached out to me in the last year. In fact, I'm reaching out to them. God is so good."

—A. A.

* * *

"A gentleman had polio as a child. He walked up with two arm brace canes on Sunday. I prayed for him and laid hands on him. He walked away the same way as he had come up. On Monday, he had physical therapy as always…and on Wednesday and on Friday.

"Yet as the physical therapist was maneuvering his leg, he complained, 'Ouch! That hurts.' The therapist examined the leg and found that his muscles were growing. He had never had muscle aches before. God has restored all the muscles to him. All the effects of polio were gone. But it took a matter of days."

—J. K.

* * *

A lady couldn't hug her son. She couldn't wear undergarments. She could hardly bear to have any clothes touch her because she hurt so badly. After prayer, she was totally and completely healed. She came back the next week to give her testimony.

However, she ended her testimony with the word "but...." Because she had been in so much pain, she had been on a lot of pain medications. She had become addicted. Always pray for the spirit of addiction! I prayed. I cursed that addiction. She never took another pain pill, and the addiction was completely gone.

* * *

A lady from Peru was in the hospital all day trying to have a kidney stone removed without anesthesia. She went home and had her husband bathe and dress her to come to the meeting. I prayed. I cursed the stone and commanded it to be dissolved. Instantly, the pain left. She said, "Excuse me," and she had to leave the platform. She eliminated the stone within a few minutes, and all the pain was gone.

* * *

While I was in Ireland, Kari's responsibility was to keep me furnished with hot tea. Because she thought God couldn't use her, she opted not to go through the class. She just wanted to be there and serve so those who were more qualified to learn how to heal the sick could learn. She took off Thursday, Friday, and Saturday. She tried to get her boss to come so he could be healed. He didn't come, but he knew she was going to a healing school.

On Monday, he came and said, "Well, Kari, how was your healing school?"

She replied, "I learned that I can do this, and you don't have to go to a healing service to get healed."

He said, "Okay, well, let's try it out. I have a bad shoulder and a bad back."

Kari prayed for him. He was instantly healed. It opened her eyes to the fact that God could use her. God had her at the meeting for more than serving hot tea!

* * *

A lady in South Carolina named Gloria came to a healing school and caught the vision that God could use her. She started praying for people, and they were getting healed. She then went to the hospital to pray for people from her church. They got healed. The church put her in charge of hospital visitation. She was one of the least likely people to be in charge of such an important position. God is using her because she made herself available to Him.

* * *

A lady from Georgia called for prayer. She had finished the healing school on the weekend and had gone back to work on Monday. She had her book on her desk. A couple of people asked her what the book was about. She told them it was on healing and that God had called her to lay hands on the sick. One of them said, "I have a bad back." She prayed. The person got healed. Another lady came in to say, "I have carpal tunnel syndrome. Can you pray for that?" Of course she could pray, and the second lady got healed, also.

Before lunchtime, her boss said, "I want to see you in my office at one o'clock." She called the church office for prayer, because she was afraid she was going to lose her job.

Her boss stood with his arms crossed and asked, "What have you been doing today?"

"Well, I have been doing accounts payable....I have been handling phone calls...."

He interrupted with, "No, what have you been doing today?" She listed her duties, and he interrupted again, "No, what have you been doing today?"

"I have been praying for some people during my break, and they have been getting healed."

"*Okay.* Well, I have this back and neck problem. Would you pray for me?"

Instead of getting fired, this woman was able pray for her boss's healing! She had been praying for a new position at her job. Two weeks later, she was promoted out of the department. When she completed the job God had for her to do and everyone was healed in her department, God promoted her into another position.

* * *

These represent only a few of the thousands of testimonies that have come into the ministry office. I now ask you...

What will your testimony be?

CHAPTER 14

Use What You Have Learned

God is healing today. This information must reach around the world to as many people as possible. He didn't impart these revelations so I could hide them and use them occasionally when I felt like it. *No!* He wants this information to be shared with everyone; it must be available for His people. He gave it to me, knowing I would share it freely. I give it to everyone I meet. It is up to you, the reader, to take this information and use it for the good of the kingdom.

Learn from Your Past, Don't Base Your Future on It

I was talking to a friend who quickly discarded the value of a person's "negative" past. She said, "If we consider our pasts in any decisions we make today, we have not given our pasts to Jesus Christ, and we are living under the curse of the past."

Personally, I believe that if we use our pasts as excuses for *not* doing what God wants us to do, then we aren't listening to God. We are listening to and succumbing to the words of the enemy. God sees so much potential in each of us. Our testimonies are basically about how God has freed us from the bondage of our pasts. The bad things that happened in the past have shaped and formed us. We don't just look at how great King David was in his younger years, hop over the middle years, and then focus on the wisdom of his later years. We study and learn from his experiences.

We should not ignore or negate the power of Jesus' blood when He wiped away our sins of the past. God

> **If we use our pasts as excuses for *not* doing what God wants us to do, then we aren't listening to God.**

may separate our sins from us, but we all know where we came from, as well as the pain of being separated from God.

God Can Use You!

I pray that you have absorbed and learned many things through these pages. Now, I have to encourage you to use what you have learned. Don't let this information lie dormant. Don't be satisfied with what you have attained. Christian growth is progressive. God always has something exciting around the next corner. If we become satisfied, then something is wrong.

You might think, *I don't have much to offer God.* Yet the smallest thing God spoke of in the Bible is a mustard seed, and it was used as an analogy for all the faith you need to start in the kingdom of God! (See Matthew 13:31–32.) I will plant a tiny mustard seed of faith in God's Word and watch it grow. It will grow into monumental faith that can do anything for God. There is no limit!

In 2 Kings 4:3–4, God wanted the widow who was caring for Elisha to fill vessels with oil, but first, she had to gather the vessels. She had to prepare to receive the harvest.

> Then [Elisha] *said, "Go, borrow vessels from everywhere, from all your neighbors; empty vessels; do not gather just a few. And when you have come in, you shall shut the door behind you and your sons; then pour it into all those vessels, and set aside the full ones."*
>
> (2 Kings 4:3–4)

It is time to get ready for what God wants us to do. Prepare for the harvest; gather your vessels and fill them with the Word of God. In 2 Kings 3:16–17, there was no water until the ditches had been dug.

> [Elisha] *said, "Thus says the LORD: 'Make this valley full of ditches.' For thus says the LORD: 'You shall not see wind, nor shall you see rain; yet that valley shall be filled with water, so that you, your cattle, and your animals may drink.'"*   (2 Kings 3:16–17)

Why would God pour out bucketfuls of blessings if we have only a cup to receive them? Lazarus would not have been resurrected if someone had not removed the stone. Standing at Lazarus' grave, Jesus said, *"Take away the stone"* (John 11:39). There had to be obedience for Lazarus to come forth.

> **There is never a harvest unless the ground has been prepared and the seed has been planted.**

There is never a harvest unless the ground has been prepared and the seed has been planted. I want to encourage you to give God your all and allow Him to utilize all your potential. You might be thinking, *But God, You know better than I that I have nothing to offer You.* God knows you have much to offer. Who are we to question God or doubt His choice for His calling?

If you truly want to do something for God, why haven't you done it? What has the enemy told you that has kept you from doing it? Whatever it is, lay it at the feet of Jesus, right now.

In the past, I have often had to deal with the fact that most people would rather have my mom and dad minister to them than me, but I know that I know that God has called me to minister, also, and not just work at the book table or sit on the platform and smile. Finally, I began to believe that people would be excited to see me and hear what I have to share. The change came in me, not in the people, when I realized, *I know that I have something good to offer.*

Do what you can do with the talents you have been given. Don't hide them. As you do with your talents what you can, God will bless them back to you.

Don't receive your healing for a heart problem, an inferiority problem, or something else and then allow the devil to steal it from you. Take a stand. Say a prayer like this one:

> In the name of Jesus, I am not inferior. Cancer has no place in me. I don't want it, and I won't receive it. Because of the empowering

of the Holy Spirit, I have recognized my potential and will do what You have called me to do, Lord! Amen.

God has called you. According to Isaiah 61:3, He has given you the oil of joy; He has given you praise; He has called you a tree of righteousness; He has planted you. What you do should glorify Him.

Give God Your Whole Heart

We need to discuss one more subject before putting all of this information to use. Understanding the following concept is very important. You may need to read it more than once to comprehend its truth. Whether you have experienced this or recognize it in someone to whom you minister, you must understand this powerful truth.

To explain, let me use the analogy of a husband and a wife. When they were courting, they freely gave their hearts to each other. A few weeks or months after the honeymoon ended, the husband did something to make his wife angry. She said she forgave him, but what he did hurt her deeply. Almost unconsciously, she took back part of her heart. She pulled away a few inches for a few days. The next time something happened, she pulled away again…and then again.

After numerous incidents over several years, she pulled back so far that she did not even recognize her husband anymore. He probably didn't know who she was, either. Neither one of them could figure out what had happened to that intimate relationship they once shared. Occasionally, I hear the comment, "We just grew apart."

After asking a few questions about any strained relationship, I can usually identify unforgiveness, anger, and resentment, which all have grown from tiny seeds of unmet expectations. In this analogy, a huge distance emerged between the husband and wife, and neither one could remember the days of happiness and oneness. The intimacy was gone. The feelings were gone. Love was nonexistent. Don't take back part of your heart.

Don't take back part of your heart.

The Word says to forgive, but the hurting wife in this example found it very difficult because she didn't trust her husband not to hurt her again. He didn't meet her expectations, and she was afraid of suffering that pain again. She protected herself, put up a wall, and pulled back from the relationship.

Like everyone else, you have learned through your experiences in life. In your youth, you could have had a crush on someone and given him a bit of your heart—whether he deserved it or not. With each deeply felt relationship, a bit of your heart was involved. Even that "Cinderella" or "Knight in Shining Armor" is capable of stealing your heart away one day and then piercing it with arrows of deceit and betrayal the next. Broken promises, hasty words, and so many other things can pierce the lover's heart and form long-lasting scars.

Through the years, little bits of your heart can be scattered across numerous relationships. We all have to gather these bits up and allow God to make our hearts whole again. If you've given your heart to another person in your life, whether an ex-spouse or one who has gone on to be with the Lord, be sure that you have your whole heart back before you get into another relationship. It's not fair for an ex-spouse from the past to keep any part of your heart.

Have you ever felt like God disappointed you? Answer honestly. Has He always met every one of your expectations? The answer is probably *no*. Did He do everything the way that you wanted him to do it every time? *No.*

Just as in the analogy of marriage partners, if God doesn't meet our expectations, we might take back parts of our hearts from Him. Not only do we take back parts of our hearts from God, but we also take back our trust and faith. Then, we are hesitant about trusting Him completely.

Many people feel like there is something missing in their relationships with God and have no idea what it is. Do you want to know what it is? You have taken back part of your heart from God!

I gave you the marriage analogy so that you could have a greater understanding of what also happens in the spirit realm. We have to choose to gather all the parts of our hearts together and return to our first love—God! He wants to have first place in your life. Does He have first place in your heart? You must go to Him with a willing heart—a heart that is totally, completely sold-out to Him.

Joshua said, *"choose today whom you will serve"* (Joshua 24:15 NLT). What happens tomorrow? You chose yesterday, so do you have to choose again today? When you read the same Scripture tomorrow, it is still going to say, *"choose today."* Read it the next day, and it will say the same thing. Will it change next week or next year? *No!*

Choose to pray:

> Father, I repent of my sins. There have been many times when I felt that You let me down. There were times when I felt like You weren't with me. I know now that You were. I took back part of my heart, and I repent of that, in Jesus' name. I choose today to give You all of my heart. I want Jesus Christ to be the Lord of my life. I don't just want to know about You, I want to know You in a personal way. Father, reveal Yourself to me on a daily basis. I want to know Your voice with no doubt. Father, I love You. Thank You, Jesus! In Your name, amen.

Use What You Have Learned

We go into the grocery store and expect to get what we pay for. We pray for the sick so that they will get what Jesus paid for. He paid the ultimate price for the salvation of the world—for you and for me. We play a vital role in this portrait of salvation and healing that God has so marvelously painted for us in His Word. Our part is not to sit on the sidelines and watch others play the game. We have to get involved and act. What are the rules? What steps can we take? It is time for all people to use what they have learned.

If you are a football player or just an avid fan, you know that when the ball is tossed to the quarterback, he doesn't just sit down where he is or fall protectively on the ball. He has to act. He has to take the next step. He has to act offensively and throw the ball to the next player.

As believers learning more and more about God's Word, we have a choice. We can use His Word or just sit down and hoard this life-saving information. God doesn't want us to play defense and fall protectively on the ball (His Word) when it is thrown our way. He wants us on the offensive, moving forward, sharing with the next player, and the next, and the next. When we get the ball (God's Word on healing), we need to run with it. The more we run with it (give it away), the more we will receive.

Guidelines for Prayer

The Lord's Prayer says, *"Our Father in heaven, hallowed be Your name. Your kingdom come. Your will be done on earth as it is in heaven"* (Matthew 6:9–10).

> **Jesus is the Healer. You are simply a willing conduit.**

In heaven, there is no lack, no sickness, no financial problems, and no stress. This is the way God wants it to be on earth. Have you ever considered the fact that God can't give you cancer? He doesn't have it to give. Jesus is the Healer. You are simply a willing conduit.

In the introduction to this book, I prayed that your eyes and ears would be opened and enlightened. Now, you may start hearing things that you have never heard before. As people walk by, you may hear their quiet groans and sighs. You may believe that your natural ears have been healed; however, it will be your spiritual ears that have been opened. You may be very sensitive to others as you hear, see, and listen beyond yourself. God will open up your heart, ears, and understanding to the needs of others.

So, how can you use what you have learned? In a moment, we will discuss some basic steps to ministry. But first, here are a few guidelines for prayer.

First, pray in the name of Jesus. Everything has to respond to His name, including diseases and illnesses. Every knee shall bow. It's that simple.

> *When He had come into the house, the blind men came to Him. And Jesus said to them, "Do you believe that I am able to do this?" They said to Him, "Yes, Lord." Then He touched their eyes, saying, "According to your faith let it be to you."* (Matthew 9:28–29)

Second, lay hands on the sick. Your ability to allow God to work through you as you lay hands on the sick is not dependent in any way on your past—especially your negative past. You don't need to beg God or say, "If it is Your will, God!" We don't have to wonder. We don't have to whimper or whine. The Bible tells us that healing *is* His will. Jesus took the stripes for our healing.

> *[Jesus] Himself bore our sins in His own body on the tree, that we, having died to sins, might live for righteousness—by whose stripes you were healed.* (1 Peter 2:24)

Third, pray specifically. You can yell and scream at a disease all you want, and you may get a response. However, you need to pray specifically for a disease "in Jesus' name" if you sincerely want results.

> *…that at the name of Jesus every knee should bow, of those in heaven, and of those on earth, and of those under the earth.*
>
> (Philippians 2:10)

Take Off the Limits!

Become what you believe. See yourself ministering to others in need. In your mind's eye, see those who will get saved, be healed, and rejoice over their miracles. See yourself sharing God's Word with confidence and peaceful assurance. Place higher standards on what you want to do with His assistance. With God, become who He wants you to become!

God wants to use you. Lay hands on the sick. See them recover. Create an opportunity for ministry. Invite someone for lunch or dinner. Visit the sick in the hospital. Hold a healing service at church or in a Bible study. Satisfy their interest. Answer their questions honestly and with God's input.

> **We are God's tools. He uses us; He works through us.**

We are God's tools. He uses us; He works through us. Where His tools go, healing flows.

A man in his late thirties came for ministry. He was paralyzed on the left side and had foot drop. After prayer, the feeling returned to his left side, his mobility came back, and he wiggled his toes for the first time in six years. He had been carried up to the platform, but he walked up and down the stairs before returning to his seat.

Another man had endured fourteen back surgeries and struggled with almost constant pain. After ministry for healing of the scar tissue from all the surgeries and replacement of all the damaged ligaments, bones, discs, and nerves, he was healed. He smiled with total relief as the pain disappeared from his body.

There are some basic steps to ministry that everyone needs to learn and understand in order to experience similar results. When ministering, follow these steps.

1. Ask.

When people come in for ministry, one of the first questions we ask is, "What do you want Jesus to do for you? What do you expect to accomplish through ministry today?" When they can identify exactly what they want, they can define those goals for whoever will minister to them. If they don't know where they want to go, neither you nor they will know when the goal has been reached.

> *So Jesus answered and said to him, "What do you want Me to do for you?" The blind man said to Him, "Rabboni, that I may receive my sight."* (Mark 10:51)

> *Then the LORD answered me and said: "Write the vision and make it plain on tablets, that he may run who reads it."* (Habakkuk 2:2)

Ask how long the disease or situation has been obvious. If it has been going on from childhood, the cause could be a generational curse. If the illness occurred a few years earlier, find out what happened within that period of time.

Often, some kind of trauma will have occurred that needs to be dealt with, such as an automobile accident, a divorce, or the death of a family member or close friend. Ask God to deal with root causes like unforgiveness or a spirit of trauma following an accident. When you hit the brakes just before your car is hit from behind, for example, fear can enter and release stress hormones that affect you in every area of your life for years to come.

> *He asked his father, "How long has this been happening to him?" And he said, "From childhood."* (Mark 9:21)

Occasionally, God will tell you what is wrong with the person who comes to you for ministry. You need to minister to the person's needs, which may be different from what your eyes tell you. For instance, the person may be in a wheelchair, but what she wants is freedom from breathing problems, not the ability to walk again.

After you get healed, you have to go back to work, and you can't take advantage of handicap parking anymore.

If the person doesn't know the details of the disease, go with your best guess. However, it is always best to get as much information as possible.

Do whatever it takes. If you need to hold notes for prayer, lay one hand on the person and read the healing prayers from the notes in your other hand. It works. It has worked around the world as believers have learned how to lay hands on the sick.

I will give a warning to those who have been or are going to be healed: after you get healed, you have to go back to work, and you can't take advantage of handicap parking anymore. That's the only "downfall" about getting healed. Then again, you can always use your handicap car marker as a bookmark!

2. Look. Watch. Pray.

Keep your eyes open and instruct those you pray for to keep their eyes open, also. Ask them to look at you while you minister to them. It is important that you look at the person for whom you are praying because the eyes will tell you what is going on in the heart.

> *And fixing his eyes on him, with John, Peter said, "Look at us." So he gave them his attention, expecting to receive something from them.*
> (Acts 3:4–5)

> *The lamp of the body is the eye. If therefore your eye is good, your whole body will be full of light. But if your eye is bad, your whole body will be full of darkness.* (Matthew 6:22–23)

Any person to whom you are ministering may be "slain in the Spirit." For those who don't know what this means, let me explain. When the power of God comes over people, they generally fall over. It is like floating gently to the floor. If someone is standing in front of a chair, she will suddenly find that she is sitting down instead of standing up. Some people are very sensitive to the anointing and are easily slain in the Spirit. Occasionally, someone will flatly refuse and brace himself against falling, only to find God has other ideas. He finds himself on the floor, looking up, and he realizes something glorious has happened to him.

When a person is slain in the Spirit, some think that the minister pushed that person over. I will admit that there are some who minister with "heavy hands"; however, I have also seen people go over with a wave of a hand or a whispering breath of air. In other words, no one touched them at all as they fell under the power of God. Sometimes, it seemed like their legs just gave out as they crumpled to the floor.

Experiences vary greatly, as well as the testimonies following. One person may immediately rise from the floor while the next may lie there for several minutes. I have seen people lie on the floor under the power of God for hours, but that is a rare occurrence. Many people get healed under this special ministry by the Holy Spirit.

Just remember to let them get slain by the Spirit and not by your strength. It is not our job to push people over. If God wants them to get slain in the Spirit, let God do it. Let God get the glory. Don't make a big deal out of whether someone gets slain in the Spirit or not. If they get slain in the Spirit, fine. If they don't and they get healed, I'd rather they get healed and give their testimonies of healing than merely falling over.

If possible, in every service, you should arrange to have someone stand behind the person receiving ministry to ease him or her safely to the floor in case he or she gets slain in the Spirit. I want to be prepared in the event that the person does get slain in the Spirit.

If you are ministering without assistance, place your hand behind the person's back. If I am praying for someone individually, I will have one hand on his or her head (if it's a head problem), but I will also have a hand behind the person, because it is my responsibility to make sure that he or she does not get hurt. In these cases, people are entrusting their lives to me; they are trusting that they won't get hurt as I pray for them.

Plan for the event that everyone will get slain in the Spirit, but don't get upset if no one does. God works differently in every group of people. If a woman wearing a dress is slain in the Spirit, quickly cover her legs with a cloth to protect her modesty. I have seen gentlemen use their suit coats when necessary. Also, it is always thoughtful to have someone assist the person up off the floor with a helping hand when he or she is ready to stand up.

After an experience of being slain in the Spirit, some feel light-headed and may need to sit for a while before trying to walk away. Some describe the feeling as being "drunk in the Spirit" because the sense of balance can be temporarily affected.

3. Listen.

There may be underlying factors that need to be handled before total healing can occur. Listen to what the people say. Listen to what they *don't* say. Hearing *how* they speak is very important, too.

For out of the abundance of the heart the mouth speaks. A good man out of the good treasure of his heart brings forth good things, and an evil man out of the evil treasure brings forth evil things.

(Matthew 12:34–35)

People don't conform only to other people or their environments; they also take on the identities of their illnesses. Sometimes, it is difficult to pray for them when they know their disabilities can get them good parking spaces. Remember my earlier warning? You will have to give up your handicapped parking permit.

For example, a woman said to me, "My friend Arthur and I need prayer. You know my friend, Arthur-itis." This lady had taken on the identity of her arthritis and claimed it as her friend. Arthritis was actually there to kill, steal, and destroy her in every area of her life.

Another example: I hate the statement, "The doctor said I have to learn to live with the pain." That is a lie from the pit of hell. We don't have to live with pain. If a doctor tells you that, you have the option of accepting it or rejecting it. Those words need to be cut off, in Jesus' name. If a doctor gives you two years to live, cut those words off, too. Choose life.

I prayed for a lady in Tulsa who explained that she was suffering with painful arthritis all over her body. After I prayed in the name of Jesus, cursed the arthritis, and commanded it to be gone in Jesus' name, I asked her, "Where is the pain?"

She said, "Nothing happened." I opted not to pray again at that point. I asked a member of the ministry team to take her to the foyer and minister to her. Within five minutes, she was totally free of pain. She

Many root causes of illness are imbedded deep within the mind and soul.

didn't need further prayer for her arthritis; ministry for unforgiveness was necessary. When the woman forgave, the arthritis disappeared.

Many root causes of illness are imbedded deep within the mind and soul. With God's wisdom, you will learn to identify these negative roots and destroy them. In their place, God's seeds of recovery, restoration, and reconciliation will be planted. These wonderful, strong, and powerful roots from great mustard seeds will enable you to do mighty things for God.

When you are ministering, you need to listen carefully. Be sensitive to the Holy Spirit telling you what the underlying cause may be. For instance, scar tissue following back surgery can be very dangerous if it is not dealt with. Many times, another surgical procedure has to be performed to remove the scar tissue caused by the initial surgery. When you are praying for someone's back, the scar tissue could be pressing against the spinal cord.

Your prayer might sound like this: "In the name of Jesus, I speak in new discs or new vertebrae. I command all the scar tissue to go." Since back injuries are often caused by trauma and open the door to fear, which worsens the condition, I will also command the spirit of trauma and fear to go.

> *I say to you that whoever is angry with his brother without a cause shall be in danger of the judgment. And whoever says to his brother, 'Raca!' shall be in danger of the council. But whoever says, 'You fool!' shall be in danger of hell fire. Therefore if you bring your gift to the altar, and there remember that your brother has something against you....*　　　　　　　　　　　　　　　　　　　(Matthew 5:22–23)

When a person comes for prayer, you may often ask yourself, *Where do I put my hand to minister to him?* He may tell you what the condition is, but if you are not medically attuned, you may lay hands on his nose for a problem in his abdomen. If you don't know where the problem is, ask the person to put his hand on the affected area of his body. Then, *if appropriate*, put your hand on his as you minister healing.

4. Relax.

Your reputation is not on the line. God's is. He will not fail. You are acting in the authority of Jesus Christ. Don't wonder *if* they are going to get healed. That shouldn't even be in your thoughts. Expect healing.

> **Your reputation is not on the line. God's is. He will not fail.**

A few days after a healing school I held in England, a lady told me about her first experience praying for someone. She was very proud but very upset at the same time. She had prayed for someone at her job, and as she did so, she had pellets of perspiration running down her face. Her hands were sweating. Instead of the anointing with living water, it was the anointing with sweat. She felt embarrassed that she had been so nervous.

I simply encouraged her to relax. Just remember: it's not by our might or our power that people are going to be healed. It is by the power of Jesus Christ living in us. He works through us as we appropriate His power, knowing His authority to minister and pray for other people. It is up to God to heal them. I do not have to worry about rejection. We give it all up to Him and let Him do it.

When I minister to people, I encourage them to relax. I also tell them to keep their eyes open and not to pray in tongues. I tell them, "Relax. Let God do it." God can heal people whether their arms are up or down. Let God's grace and anointing do the work. Don't try to make the healing happen. Just allow God to do it.

> *Trust in the LORD with all your heart, and lean not on your own understanding; in all your ways acknowledge Him, and He shall direct your paths.* (Proverbs 3:5–6)

Earlier, we prayed through the prophetic word that your eyes and ears would be opened to hear God more clearly, and that you would walk in greater wisdom and knowledge than you have ever walked in before. If you do not know how to pray for a situation, don't stop ministering. God can override your natural mind, whether you have this book readily available for reference or not.

This book includes methods and prayers that have been successful through my years in ministry. I have not included anything that hasn't worked in the past. I want you to pray with confidence for the sick just as God has commissioned all believers to do. If you don't know what to do or say, ask Him. Ask God for a word of knowledge.

One time in England, I was praying for a man who explained, "When I eat, I can't breathe. My food goes down into my lungs."

In the natural, I was trying to understand. I asked, "Do you have a hole in your esophagus?"

He said that all the examinations and diagnostic tests had showed nothing abnormal. Well, God knew what was wrong. I had a vision of his esophagus. Every time he ate, a bubble appeared. My daughter, Spice, MD, ND, was on this trip with me, and I turned to her and asked, "Is there such as thing as a herniated esophagus? I have never heard of that."

She confirmed the revelation as an authentic diagnosis. I said, "That is what I see—a herniated esophagus. It does not have a hole, but when he eats, his esophagus bubbles out like bubble gum. It bulges out. Food gets stuck there and blocks his passageway so he can't breathe."

When I got a glimpse of the problem in the spirit realm, I could proceed. In the name of Jesus, I spoke in a whole new esophagus. He had pain in his chest. When I commanded the pain to go, the pain left instantly. Before the ministry team left England, he had enjoyed three perfect meals with no complications. God gave him a new esophagus.

New diseases and conditions are always being identified. Many of them are developing because of the increased stress in our lives, which is due to the complex, fast-paced modern world and the poor quality of food we are putting into our bodies.

Another young man came to me for prayer. He had passed a kidney stone several years before. Since then, he had experienced many problems. There was some kind of blockage. I prayed and had a vision of a passageway filled with scar tissue. The stone had caused residual scar tissue that was blocking the passage of urine. I commanded all the scar tissue to go, in Jesus' name. When we saw the young man three days later, he reported that he was fine. The problem was completely gone.

When someone explains his or her problems and you aren't at all sure how to pray, depend on God to give you the answer—whether with a vision, a prophetic word, or a word of knowledge. Be sensitive to His voice. Depend on hearing from the Lord about what to say.

Wait on the Lord. Listen to His leading.

Wait on the Lord. Listen to His leading. *"Wait on the Lord; be of good courage, and He shall strengthen your heart; wait, I say, on the Lord!"* (Psalm 27:14).

5. Don't Quit.

Jesus prayed twice for a blind man. Talk to the person. Ask God for discernment. Figure out what is blocking the healing. Sometimes, it takes more than one prayer. Ask for more specific details. Don't quit. Someone once asked, "If I don't get healed the first time, should I come back for prayer again?" I don't have a problem with that at all. Do whatever works—pray until something happens, pray until you get healed. Do whatever it takes.

He came to Bethsaida; and they brought a blind man to Him, and begged Him to touch him. So He took the blind man by the hand and led him out of the town. And when He had spit on his eyes and put His hands on him, He asked him if he saw anything. And he looked up and said, "I see men like trees, walking." Then He put His hands on his eyes again and made him look up. And he was restored and saw everyone clearly. (Mark 8:22–25)

Be confident. Know that it is God's will to heal. Be the message you bring. Know that what you do speaks louder than what you say. Follow God's leading. Just talking to people in general will make them fall asleep. But talk to their hearts, speak to their souls, and they will live.

Don't give up. Some people won't accept your ministry or your words of healing. Remember, some people rejected Jesus, also. Not one of us is better than He. Just take a deep breath and say, "*Next?*" with full confidence that God is directing your words and your actions. He is the One you have to answer to.

6. Give Thanks!

Give God the glory! Instruct those you pray for to say, "Thank You, Jesus!" Before they test their healings, they should give Him thanks. Praise Jesus! Thank Him for the miracle of healing that has occurred. Thank Him, even if the outward manifestation has not appeared yet. Just give Him all the glory, all the praise, and all your appreciation.

Rejoice always, pray without ceasing, in everything give thanks; for this is the will of God in Christ Jesus for you.
(1 Thessalonians 5:16–18)

Have an attitude of gratitude! That attitude will flavor everything you do. Give God thanks immediately and instruct those around you to do so, also.

Have an attitude of gratitude! It will flavor everything you do.

The enemy will want to bring back the symptoms in an attempt to cancel a healing. Offering praise and thanksgiving is the best way to maintain the miracle of healing. Instruct those who have been healed to search out the Scriptures and keep God's promises in front of them. Again, it is a choice—a choice to believe God's promises or the lies of the enemy, who wants to keep a person in bondage to sickness and death. Make the right choice.

Everyone ministers in his or her own way; however, these are the steps that I have found to be successful in my ministry. They are the way God has shown me to pray. If you do it differently, will people get healed? Probably. With experience, you will develop your own way, which will fit your personality, and you will carry out what God tells you to do.

Like I've done in this book, many Christian leaders will explain the steps by which they have reached their level of spiritual wisdom and insight into God's Word. I'm not saying that anyone is wrong; however, I will caution you from attempting to copy another person's actions in all cases. God uses different methods with different people, but in every situation, He wants your obedience.

So, remember: you are not going to do everything the same way I do. You can follow me while you are learning, but God doesn't want you to mimic me or anyone else forever. He wants you to listen to His voice and obey His instructions.

As miracles start to manifest in your ministry, don't ever forget to give Him all the glory. You can share your exciting experiences with me. I love to hear what happens when other believers learn what I teach and use it to further His work.

Healing was a way of life for Jesus. It should be a way of life for all of us, also.

CHAPTER 15

Anoint Me, Lord

The Spirit of the LORD is upon Me, because He has anointed Me to preach the gospel to the poor; He has sent Me to heal the broken-hearted, to proclaim liberty to the captives and recovery of sight to the blind, to set at liberty those who are oppressed; to proclaim the acceptable year of the LORD. (Luke 4:18–19)

You have an anointing from the Holy One, and you know all things.... But the anointing which you have received from Him abides in you, and you do not need that anyone teach you; but as the same anointing teaches you concerning all things, and is true, and is not a lie, and just as it has taught you, you will abide in Him. (1 John 2:20, 27)

Many people do not understand what the anointing is or what it can do in their lives. Even the dictionary doesn't explain the anointing as it is interpreted in today's Christian world. The dictionary authors consider it a verb, an action, e.g., "to bless somebody with oil, to rub oil or ointment on a part of somebody's body as part of a religious ceremony," or "to ordain, to install somebody officially or ceremonially in a position or office."

From studying the original language, we find that the translation of *Christ* is "the anointed one," from which the English *Messiah* is derived. The Hebrew concept of anointing came from the ancient belief that the application of oil endowed the person or object with certain superior and even supernatural qualities. In early Israel, the custom of anointing with oil signified the blessing of the person with the qualifications for exalted office. For example, Samuel anointed David to be king. (See 1 Samuel 16:1–13.)

In the New Testament, the word *Christ* became the designation of Jesus of Nazareth as the expected Messiah of the Jews. This name has remained through the centuries as the English application of the term.

Using the Anointing Today

You may understand the anointing as a rite of the church, but we are going to delve deeper into this amazing and life-changing practice as it relates to all believers today. You can experience it in your everyday life, as well as when you minister God's love and healing to others.

You can experience the anointing in your everyday life, as well as when you minister God's love and healing to others.

I'll share with you some ideas and thoughts about how to increase the anointing in your life—whether you are ministering in the pulpit, one-on-one, or just in the privacy of your own home. It doesn't make any difference where you are or what you are doing. God is omnipresent. Because He is always there, you can tap into and walk in His anointing wherever you go.

How can you enjoy and participate in His anointing? It is simple. If you are saved, Jesus lives within you. This means that you are *"in Christ"* (Romans 8:1), or "in the Anointed One," and you share in His anointing.

You have to allow and welcome Him and His anointing into your life. God will not force His anointing onto you or anyone else. Some people will attend a service with a negative attitude and resist everything about God. Will they feel His anointing? No. However, if you open your heart to God and yearn for more of Him, you will be able to feel Him working through you. Because God is omnipresent, He is all around us at all times. People separate themselves from Him with negative attitudes, disbelief, and sin. God doesn't leave us. We leave Him.

One person may be a great theologian with great insights into the Word of God. He may spend years studying the Bible; however, his teaching may be difficult to follow and may get boring after a short period of time. The next person spends hours searching for God's heart and is totally open to God's instructions. She makes herself available and allows God's anointing to work through her.

With such a leader, an audience can sit for hours, just soaking in a teacher's anointed message from God. They may feel like the teacher has "read their mail." In other words, the speaker's message answers questions the listeners have been wondering about or praying about. I have known pastors and teachers to rip up their prepared notes and allow God to speak through them spontaneously. That takes a sensitive spirit and great faith, but oh, it is a marvelous experience to know that God can work and speak through you in that way!

Has it happened to me? Yes, it has. Suddenly, I have found myself speaking words that have surprised even me. I have suddenly known something that I didn't know before. Call it a word of wisdom. Call it discernment. Call it hearing from God. I know it is His anointing, His Holy Spirit speaking through me. Frequently, I have listened to the tape of a service at a later date and heard things I don't remember saying. It is a unique, wonderful experience to know that God can work through you without your human interference.

Another person might sing or play an instrument. One person might sing beautifully but won't keep your attention. An anointed musician can bring an entire congregation into God's throne room within moments of starting a song. While he ministers music, he also allows God to work through him. He may indeed have incredible talent, but with God working through him, his talent explodes into so much more.

Many people throughout the years have received the anointing for healing. God has truly anointed me in that area. Does everyone get healed? Not yet. But I do open myself up to God's will. I will pray for anyone when God directs me to pray. I will lay hands on the sick and allow God's healing power and anointing to flow through my hands and into the believer. And the sick are healed.

My parents have God's healing anointing on their lives. For almost four decades, I have witnessed thousands healed, saved, and filled with the Holy Spirit under their anointing. They were open vessels, willing to let God work through their hands and voices as they traveled around the world.

I remember my parents often ministering in new, unique ways. Occasionally, they would step on someone's toes when the toes or foot needed healing. God's healing power flowed through their toes, as well as their hands. My dad would occasionally have those who wanted to be healed follow him across the platform. Why? Because God's miracles *"will follow those who believe"* (Mark 16:17).

Charles, my dad, also used the example that those who were seeking healing had to draw on the healing anointing that flowed from him. The person wanting to be healed needed to "suck" God's healing power, using Charles as a conduit. It is easy to minister to a congregation of people who are seeking, searching, and wanting something from God. They are open and expecting. I tell people to push their "expector button" if they want a miracle. Expect God to work, expect a miracle, and draw the anointing from the man or woman of God who is ministering. The results can be amazing.

> **Expect God to work, expect a miracle, and draw the anointing from the man or woman of God who is ministering.**

In today's world, we all know that a lamp can't shed light unless someone flips the switch. There has to be a connection from the source of power to the lightbulb in order for the lamp to fill the room with light. Likewise, when someone wants something from God, there has to be a connection, a conduit. You can be that connection between God and the hurting person working next to you at your job. You can turn the light on in your church as you share God's love and healing power with the sick and lonely. Are you willing to let God use you?

Are You Willing to Go Anywhere?

I want to challenge you with a few questions. With each question, I want you to stop reading and consider your answer carefully and prayerfully. Your answer shouldn't come quickly. Ponder, think, and pray. Don't give an answer based on your emotions. I want your answers to come from your heart.

Do you want to go to heaven to worship and praise God for eternity? Or do you want to go to heaven just because you don't want to go to hell? Do you want to do just barely enough to slide into heaven at the last minute because you don't want to give up your present lifestyle? Maybe you want to go to heaven to have total peace, but you aren't sure about spending an eternity with God. You don't know if you want to worship the Lord and spend time with Him forever.

Back to the present. Do you want to be used by God? I believe that every believer would answer *yes* to that question. However, at what cost?

There are several ways to look at this question. When I ask it, most people say, "Yes, I want to be used by God!" They believe they will travel around the world, meet wonderful people, and have glamorous lives as they work for an awesome God.

You hear about the ministry and how great it is to work for God. You see ministers of the gospel, teachers, and traveling evangelists on television, and you think they must have carefree, wonderful lives. What you don't hear or see is the work of the ministry that goes on behind the scenes. It's not just a matter of ministering on the platforms, in churches, at conventions or crusades, on the radio, or in front of a camera, wearing beautiful clothes and looking your best.

What if somebody calls and invites you to minister in her church? Someone wants to hear what God has given you. Excitement pours over you! However, she is calling from some place on the other side of the globe. I've actually been scheduled to go to places that I had never heard of. I've had to dig out an atlas to find out where certain churches were located.

To plan appropriately, you have to know how many people they expect to attend the meeting. Will they pay your way or expect you to handle the expenses? Do they guarantee a specific amount of money for the meetings, or will it be a freewill offering? What kind of meeting are they planning? Is it a one-day meeting, or will it last for many days? Maybe they want you to come for a month.

I have many people working for the ministry who depend on me to use godly wisdom to bring in the needed finances to pay their salaries and the other expenses of the ministry. What do I do? I pray. I seek God for His perfect will. Does God want me to go to this place? Is it God's plan or just my ego responding to this invitation? Through experience, I know that not every invitation is part of God's will.

Once I know that God is calling me to minister to a specific group, hours and hours of planning follow. Then, excitement takes over, and I use Internet search engines to research the details. I want to know the average temperatures of the climate, what clothes are necessary, and what type of cuisine will be served. The favorite meal for special guests might be monkey brains fresh out of a live monkey. That is not my favorite food.

This example is not a fictional story. Monkeys are served in Indonesia to honor the missionaries who visit there. A friend told me about the tables designed specifically for serving live monkey brains, the delicacy they provide for their special guests. The expressions on the missionaries' faces as they dine on such exquisite cuisine are priceless.

Research might show that the insects common to that country can be as large as my hand. I have small hands, but that would be a big bug. The usual sleeping arrangements might include windows with no screens. The ministry team may have to sleep under a net in a room with no air conditioning. It might be practically guaranteed that things will crawl over us as we lay on a bed of stone with nice stone pillows. Do you still want to be used of God? Perhaps you aren't quite so anxious to volunteer.

You might put some boundaries on your willingness to serve. You might want to go only to England or New York, where you won't have to sleep with the bugs or eat monkey brains. Many hesitate to open up to God's will because they are afraid to travel to the other side of the world. If God calls you to go somewhere strange, know that He will provide everything for you and bless you all along the way. However, He may not ask you to do more than go to the grocery store down on the corner and talk to the cashier. He wants to see willingness and obedience in the little things before He will challenge you or bless you with the bigger things.

I have gone to the grocery store and ministered. I have followed His leading in airports and on elevators. I have tried very hard to go and do whatever He has asked. However, I haven't been to Indonesia yet, so I can't tell you what monkey brains taste like. God has not called me there yet; but praise God for the teaching materials that can go in my stead!

Are You Willing to Give Up Everything?

Are you willing to pay the price for the ministry and for His anointing? One of my children told me, "Mom, I really want to be in the ministry, but I do not want to pay the price that you've paid." I understand that attitude. My children have lived through and watched my journey. I have paid a high price to do what God is calling me to do and to stand up for what is right.

The question is, are you willing to pay the price? How much are you willing to pay? How much does it cost? The price is not measured in money. God sometimes requires you to give up everything—whether it is your home, finances, job, or security—but He certainly does not require everyone to give away everything, nor does He necessarily take away everything. More often, it is the intangible things He wants us to leave behind.

It is the intangible things He wants us to leave behind.

If you do lose or give things up for Him and His work, know that He will bless you back with much more than you could ever fathom. What would you

192

do if God asked you to give up your home, your family, or your childhood dreams? To give up vacations and television? What if He asked you to give up the most precious thing in your life? What would you do to fill your time if all those precious people or things were gone?

Do you remember the woman with the alabaster jar?

Being in Bethany at the house of Simon the leper, as [Jesus] sat at the table, a woman came having an alabaster flask of very costly oil of spikenard. Then she broke the flask and poured it on His head.

(Mark 14:3)

Later in this passage, Jesus said that the woman's action was to *"anoint My body for burial"* (verse 8). Unknowingly, this woman was preparing Jesus' body for burial, even though He was still alive. Although this woman had done something absolutely incredible, some people present were indignant at her flagrant "waste" of oil, which represented more than an entire year's worth of income.

What are you doing with your money, your income, your social security, or your 401(k)? Perhaps God has told you to give it away. Be careful whom you tell. You may get a positive response; too often, however, you will get a negative comment. "What are you thinking? You are crazy!" You're probably going to have people rise up against you, just like they came against the woman with the alabaster jar. They are going to say negative things and misunderstand your obedience to God's instructions.

After co-pastoring for eighteen years, I have learned this lesson time and again. If you do a good deed, someone else will probably get upset. In his or her eyes, the money (oil) should have gone into the building fund or toward the children's department instead of being "wasted." These people won't understand your heart—just like they did not understand her heart. She was grateful for all that God had done for her. The critics did not know that by doing this, the woman was preparing Jesus for His burial.

No matter what you do, it's not going to make everybody happy. Get

> **The only One we all need to please is God.**

that settled and out of the way. *The only One we all need to please is God.*

No matter what the cost, the woman with the alabaster jar gave freely and with her whole heart. That's what Jesus wants. He wants us to give Him our all—whether it is our finances, our time, our minds, or our bodies. He doesn't want 10 percent anymore; He wants 100 percent.

God Will Give You the Strength

Romans 10:14–15 asks how can people hear, know, or believe in Jesus unless someone is sent to them to tell them. I love that Scripture. Do you want to be sent? You might be sent to Ireland or England and stay in a five-star hotel. Then again, you might end up in less comfortable circumstances.

Some people think that a cheap hotel is no better than camping out. But what happens when you find that your bedroom is literally the open air, with bugs and creepy crawlers, and that the washing machine is the river? No five-star hotel. No hair spray, no shampoo, no bottled water, no showers, no ice, no air conditioning, and no heat. Maybe no bathrooms whatsoever.

I am not cut out for tents, netting, bugs, or monkeys, but I know that God will give me the grace and strength to do whatever is necessary to fulfill His will and His calling. Understand that working in the ministry is not all glamour and comfort.

While we were ministering in Berlin, Germany, I had to contact the office via a local Internet café. My husband, Kelley, protected me while I was online. Why? Because people were rioting outside the window, just ten feet away from where I was sitting. There was blood everywhere. Prayers of protection did their powerful work that day.

Lord, look on their threats, and grant to Your servants that with all boldness they may speak Your word, by stretching out Your hand to heal, and that signs and wonders may be done through the name of Your holy Servant Jesus. (Acts 4:29–30)

God wants to work signs and wonders through everyone. That includes you. My life is anointed, and I walk in His anointing day and night. I am confident of that. I opened up my heart, arms, and life to Him years ago. I may not entirely understand His ways, but I have learned to be obedient to His voice.

I guard the anointing in the best way I know how. On a daily basis, I am in awe that God has anointed me. There are no words that can describe how I feel about His call to have a worldwide ministry. I am very careful with the privilege. I will not play with it or make fun of it. I want to guard the anointing on my life. I don't want to lose it in any way, shape, or form. It is so precious.

God gave me an answer one day when I was reading His Word: *"I am like a green olive tree in the house of God; I trust in the mercy of God forever and ever"* (Psalm 52:8).

I had been trying to protect myself and protect the anointing. I realized that the olive tree represents the oil for His anointing. God Himself protects the anointing on my life. I can't do it, but He can.

It is up to me to live a godly, sin-free life as best as I can and as much as is humanly possible, but it is up to Him to protect the anointing from other people, other situations, and anything else that could happen. All I have to do is trust Him, listen to His voice, and keep my heart pure before Him. I make that choice every day of my life.

> **There is a time of preparation before anyone is ready to answer God's call.**

There is a time of preparation before anyone is ready to answer His call. I believe that everybody can and should be used of God on a daily basis. However, a person cannot just jump in with both feet without first preparing to receive His anointing. Read His

Word, pray, and listen to Him. In other words, get as close to Him as you possibly can. Be sensitive to His call, His voice. He wants to use you. *"Be diligent to present yourself approved to God"* (2 Timothy 2:15).

God will open doors, even if you can't leave your home. A busy mother with small children or a homebound grandma may feel limited in her opportunities to minister. If you are in such a position, know that God can and will send people to you. A car can break down right outside your house. The driver may come to your door needing to borrow your phone, and you'll give him Jesus. Your next phone call may be an opportunity from God, not just an irritating sales call. Be assured that God will provide opportunities for you to share His love. Even if you can't leave your house, God will send people to you. Just be ready.

Prepare Yourself

In order to enter a higher realm and a deeper walk with the Lord, willing preparation is necessary. Just like a newborn baby can't travel around the world, neither can a newborn in ministry go everywhere at once. You must crawl before you walk and walk before you run. If you try to go around the world while in the infant stage of your ministry, you may last only a few months before devastation thwarts your plans. Prepare. Don't jump out before God says you are ready. Don't get ahead of Him.

> *Each young woman's turn came to go in to King Ahasuerus after she had completed twelve months' preparation, according to the regulations for the women, for thus were the days of their preparation apportioned: six months with oil of myrrh, and six months with perfumes and preparations for beautifying women.* (Esther 2:12)

Esther and the other maidens wanted to be acceptable in the king's sight. They were willing to spend twelve months in preparation for just one chance with the king. Can you imagine passing endless days doing nothing but preparing your mind and body in order to be allowed to spend a few hours with the king?

Today is our time of preparation as we saturate ourselves in the anointing, in His Word. We all want to serve God in a greater way than ever before, but there are steps we must take and preparations to be made before we can be used by our heavenly Father. We represent Him. He has to trust us, just like we have to believe and trust Him. He has to know that we will be faithful with little before He will trust us with much.

During one road trip, somebody told me that she really felt she was supposed to be traveling and ministering. She went on, "But please tell me that you're not human."

I asked, "What? Of course, I'm human. What do you mean?"

"Please tell me you never have a bad day, never get sick, and never have to think about your finances."

I replied, "I wish I could say that, but I can't." As a matter of fact, I had been sick and dizzy during the meeting that very day. It had been difficult for me to function.

When I had walked onto the platform that morning, one of the team members had to help me to make sure I didn't hit the wall. I got to the pulpit, the anointing hit, and people were healed all over the building. It was absolutely incredible. But when I walked off the platform, I was dizzy again. The special anointing to preach had come and gone.

I am human. I have to deal with being physically tired and frustrated. I catch myself thinking about finances and the work back home in the office. Tension increases, my shoulders get tighter, and my neck starts to hurt. I could allow all these physical symptoms to grow and finally paralyze me. It is my choice. I could give up and say, "It's too much!" I could run back home and curl up in my bed.

No! I have to dig in my heels and stay determined to carry on with God's call. I schedule a relaxing massage from the Holy Spirit: "In the name of Jesus, I lay the finances of this ministry at Your altar. I lay my tiredness at Your altar."

When I give it to God, the pain in my neck and upper back leaves. I can physically tell when I start carrying too much of the natural world around with me. But God didn't say my assignment would be easy; He said I would make it *through* the valley of the shadow of death. Yes, *"death"* is in that Scripture. (See Psalm 23:4.)

It is a fight. However, I've made it through. I learned so much going through that valley. The reality is that I am human; I have good days, I have bad days, and when I'm away and my husband Kelley can't travel with me, my heart hurts. I can't say *no* to what God has called me to do. First, God doesn't want me to do that, and second, Kelley doesn't want me to do that. I have the blessing of my husband when I need to travel without him.

> For if you remain completely silent at this time, relief and deliverance will arise for the Jews from another place, but you and your father's house will perish. Yet who knows whether you have come to the kingdom for such a time as this? (Esther 4:14)

Personally, I don't want God to choose anybody else to do my job. I do, however, believe that I am God's second choice for the call I received; I think His first choice refused the call and denied God's vision for his or her life. I'm ready and willing, and that's what is important. I chose to answer God, and I daily choose to keep following Him and listening for His next instruction.

Today, I don't want God to raise up anybody else for my job. I want to be it. I want His anointing to pour all over me and through me. I want all the things God wants me to do to land on me.

God wants us to be willing to sacrifice our lives like Esther did in the process of preparing for the king.

God wants us to be willing to sacrifice our lives like Esther did in the process of preparing for the king. By going into the king's presence without his direct invitation, she knew that he could have legally killed her—he could have just lopped off her head without even batting an eye. Knowing that her life could be over in a moment, she exercised her faith and chose to walk in the favor of God. He raised her up. She was a willing vessel. God used her. She became the queen and was instrumental in saving her people from destruction.

I want to do and experience all that God has for me. I don't want to get in His way. I want to encourage you not to get in the way of the call of God on your life—or anybody else's life, for that matter.

"Choose for yourselves this day whom you will serve....But as for me and my house, we will serve the LORD" (Joshua 24:15). Choose you today, tomorrow, and every other day whom you will serve. As for me, Joan Hunter, and my house, we will serve the Lord. It is a daily decision, not a onetime whim, and it is very important. I have greater determination today than I have ever had in my entire life. I choose Him.

Keep Growing

So, what did I tell the person who asked me if I was human? I told her that through all the situations I have encountered, God has made me stronger. Today, I thank God for every situation I have lived through. Those challenges, the bad and the good, have made me who I am today. I rejoice in God's love. He is my Creator. He has led me, loved me, and developed me into someone He can use.

Some situations occur to make you stronger. Situations will always arise, but it is up to you what you do with them. A successful man is a man who chooses to get up and keep going. He learns from his experiences and doesn't allow them to destroy him. He chooses to continue on life's path.

To paraphrase Genesis 50:20, things that were meant for evil, God has turned around for my good. This is a tremendous statement. As you consider the different situations and experiences in your life, ask God, "Why? What was my part in it? What did I do to bring this on?" Watch and be aware of how God will turn your situation around and make a miracle out of it. If you are willing and open, you are allowing Him to do marvelous things.

We know that all things work together for good to those who love God, to those who are the called according to His purpose.

(Romans 8:28)

For the Lord GOD will help Me; therefore I will not be disgraced; therefore I have set My face like a flint, and I know that I will not be ashamed. (Isaiah 50:7)

Flint is the same mineral found in Mount Rushmore. The famous faces carved from flint are literally set in stone. Even though they occasionally get some maintenance repair, they are basically unmovable, unchangeable. We need to be the same in our faith—unmovable.

A believer's pity party shouldn't last long.

One day, I was having a pity party, and I was the only one invited. A believer's pity party shouldn't last long. You have to recognize what is happening and make your choice. Whom do you believe? During my pity party, negative thoughts bombarded me. I cried out to my Daddy. "Father, who am I that You would call and anoint me? Who am I to fulfill Your call on my life? God, I don't know how I'm going to do it. I don't think I can. How can I? Why did You pick me?" I felt like everything was way too big for me to handle. Anyone being used of God will have these same thoughts from time to time.

I kept arguing with God, "Who am I?" God always wins, of course. In His still, small voice, He said, "I am the One who has called you and anointed you. I am the One who has appointed you. No matter what you or anybody else says, I am the One who has appointed and anointed you. That's all you need to know."

Just like everyone else, I have experienced rebuke and criticism. I have heard people say that I'm just not good enough to do what I do. There is nothing scriptural to back up those words. The Word doesn't say you must have a degree to qualify for His work. The Scriptures simply say that you have to believe. (See Mark 16:16–18.) Believe, be baptized, and stretch forth your hand in obedience; it's up to God to do the rest. He does the healing. His Word doesn't say that people will *probably* get healed; it instructs believers—you and me—to lay hands on the sick, assuring us that they *will* recover. They *will* be healed.

At one time, I was so afraid of making God look bad that I hesitated. I realize now that it is not my responsibility to work the miracles; it is His. One night, I opened my Bible to read, *"I have the highest confidence in you, and I take great pride in you"* (2 Corinthians 7:4 NLT). It was as if God had sat down next to me and said, "You go, girl! I am so proud of you!"

We all need that vote of confidence from our parents, from people around us whom we respect. "You are doing great! I have all the confidence in the world where you're concerned." We need to hear that from God, also. Read 2 Corinthians 7:4 again. God is speaking those words to you.

How Do You Know What God Wants You to Do?

Many of you know who my mother is. You may have heard her teaching tapes or attended her meetings. If you suddenly heard her voice, you would recognize it and know you were listening to Frances Hunter. She has a very distinctive voice.

If I announced that we were going to do a seminar on "Knowing the Voice of Your Mother," you would think it was ridiculous. If your mom called on the phone, you would know her voice immediately. She doesn't have to identify herself. You don't need any training to know her voice. Why? Because you already know her voice; you talk to her frequently; you have had an intimate relationship with her since you were born. It is so familiar to you that you recognize her voice immediately.

The same thing goes for God. The more you get to know Him and spend time with Him, the easier it is to recognize His voice. You know and recognize His voice immediately. You can differentiate between your Father's voice and the enemy's voice, which is trying to feed you lies, because of your intimate relationship with your heavenly Daddy. We don't need a seminar to learn how to recognize our mothers' voices.

We do, however, need to spend time with God and allow Him to speak to us. The better we know Him, the easier it is to recognize His voice.

Genesis 32:24–30 tells us about Jacob spending time alone with God. Jacob got away from everything and everyone to seek the Lord. During that time of separation, God visited him.

We, too, need to get away, especially with our hectic work schedules. Each of us needs to separate from the world to be alone with God. However, spending the weekend at a hotel that has 342 television channels to surf through is not what I would call getting away to spend time with the Lord. It is just time spent with the TV. No one needs to separate himself to spend time with the TV. However, everyone needs to spend time with the Lord and communicate with Him.

Talk to Him like He is right beside you, because that is exactly where He is. He is your best Friend, your forever Friend. "Here I am in this situation; what do You want me to do? I'm trying to fulfill my responsibilities in my job; what do You want me to do?" He will give you the answers you seek.

> *For in the time of trouble He shall hide me in His pavilion; in the secret place of His tabernacle He shall hide me; He shall set me high upon a rock.* (Psalm 27:5)

Even in the storms of life, you can pray to God:

> *Father, I want to do Your will. What do You want for my life? I have dreams and visions, and I lay them at Your altar. These are things that I want to do for You and things I want for my family. I thank You that in Your perfect timing, they will come to fruition. Amen.*

You Must Change to Grow

God also says that we all have to change in order to go to the next level with Him. Whoops! Everybody loves change, right? *No!* "Oh, ask me to do anything, but don't talk about change. Please, don't ask me to change!"

When a couple gets married, the husband often says that he doesn't want his wife ever to change, while the wife wants to change everything about her husband. Usually, it turns out the other way around. The woman is the one who constantly changes. If you enter into a marriage with neither partner willing to change, the marriage is doomed to fail. If one partner is willing to change but the other isn't, the marriage is still not going to be successful. Both partners have to be willing to change or compromise.

The same thing is true where God is concerned. Everyone needs to be willing to change. Being determined to do things your way or "no way" will never bring God's blessings or anointing on your projects or actions. A relationship with God means cooperation and willingness to listen to His way of doing things. If you put all of yourself into something and leave Him out entirely, there is no compromise, no open communication, and no assistance from the One with all the right answers.

> *Let the Spirit change your way of thinking and make you into a new person. You were created to be like God, and so you must please him and be truly holy.* (Ephesians 4:23–24 CEV)

We all need attitude corrections at times. For God to really use us and take us where He needs us to be, we must be willing to accept and welcome His corrections. Not only does He say that you need to change, but He also says that you should be constantly changing for the better. Constantly changing indicates an ongoing process, not just a onetime occurrence. You need to be willing to allow God to smooth out the rough edges in your life. Ask God to reveal what you need to do to take care of yourself—not the problems someone else may have exhibited. You take care of you, and God will take care of the other people in your life.

You take care of you, and God will take care of the other people in your life.

> *Then we will no longer be immature like children. We won't be tossed and blown about by every wind of new teaching. We will not be*

influenced when people try to trick us with lies so clever they sound like the truth. Instead, we will speak the truth in love, growing in every way more and more like Christ, who is the head of his body, the church. (Ephesians 4:14–15 NLT)

Instead of being tossed to and fro, we need to act and react more like Christ on a daily basis. When Joseph was in prison, he got called to the palace—but he didn't just go as he was. *"He shaved, changed his clothing, and came to Pharaoh"* (Genesis 41:14). He prepared himself for his visit with the king.

Sometimes, we need to change not only inwardly, but outwardly, too. For example, in the natural realm on ground level, maybe you can wear whatever you want to work. Your employer may not care if you wear cutoff jeans or ripped shirts. However, if you want to be the president of the company, you have to clean up your act. So what are you doing to get there? Lying around every day, talking to everybody, and wasting your employer's time and money? If so, guess again—you aren't moving up any ladder. Instead, you'll probably be ushered to the door.

If you are looking for a promotion, you need to be studying for it, looking and acting the part long before you are considered to move upward. If you want a promotion, fulfill the position you have and do it as well as you possibly can. If you want a promotion—financially or title wise—you need to be doing the work and having the attitude necessary to fulfill that position. There are many people who want promotions, but they are not willing to put in the work to obtain them.

Maybe you are a deacon in the church, but you want to be an elder. In order to become an elder, you need to be doing the job of an elder. The elders are responsible for taking care of and praying for the people. What are you doing? Are you calling the pastor to ask if there is anything you can do for him? Are you telling your family and pastor that you are praying for them and standing behind them? After doing the job, you may get the title of an elder.

For example, I have traveled with and assisted my parents for years.

In their later years in the ministry, I took care of their book table. On occasion, I did the announcements and took care of the finances. Soon, I was in charge of more details while they were on the road. As the years passed, they gave me the microphone more often. They couldn't always move down among the people, and they would ask me to pray for those seeking a touch from God.

Progressively, I got to the point where I was doing what I am doing now with my parents sitting on the platform. I was already doing what I was destined to do, what I was in the process of being promoted to do. I had to be willing to do whatever it takes. Are you?

Be Willing to Do Anything for God

At the ministry office, we have a wall that is designated for hats—any kind of hat you can imagine. We have really nice hats, and we are always looking for more interesting additions to our wall. We have cowboy hats, pink hats, feather hats, you name it. Why in the world do we have hats on our wall? Working in a ministry, everyone has to be willing to wear many hats! Everyone has to do willingly whatever has to be done, no matter what hat it requires.

What do I do for the ministry? I teach, I lay hands on the sick, I travel the world, I take out the trash, and I clean the toilets. I have done all kinds of things. If the room needs to be vacuumed, I vacuum. If there's trash on the floor, I pick it up. I've often emptied the wastebaskets when they have gotten too full.

What do I do at home? Do I just walk into a house that stays immaculately clean all the time? No. I do laundry. I cook. I do dishes. I do whatever it takes. I have to wear whatever hat is required at the time. I have to be willing—whether it means staying in the five-star hotel in New York City or sleeping on a rock in Indonesia.

Whatever it is, you have to be willing to do what needs to be done. Are you willing? Is it a nine-to-five job? The answer to that question is a resounding *no!* When God calls you into the ministry, no matter where your paycheck comes from, it is a 24-hours-a-day, 7-days-a-week, 365-days-a-year commitment. On leap years, it is 366 days.

Does that mean that I don't believe in vacations? Oh, I believe in vacations more than you know. I believe in getting away and spending quality time with my husband, my children, and the Lord. I plan these special times with family because they are important to me, but God's desires for my life and time always come first. He always goes on vacation with me and often ministers peace and restoration to my body, soul, and spirit.

> **The ministry is all about doing whatever needs to be done at the time.**

As I talked with a pastor recently, I asked her what she did at the church. She explained, "Well, one day, I may do the yard, and the next, I'll help out in the nursery. Basically, I do whatever needs to be done." She knew what the ministry is all about—doing whatever needs to be done at the time. You may have to sweep the floor, arrange chairs, set up the book table, or tear it down. Working in the ministry is not just about the good things, like ministering healing or teaching. It includes everything. That's just the way it is.

An elder can't say, "I'm not going to do that job. That's the deacon's job. I'm not going to lower myself to the position of the deacon." That elder will probably not be an elder much longer with that kind of an attitude. God will deal with that pride. God doesn't like pride or disobedience. You have to be willing to do whatever God tells you to do. No job in the ministry is beneath me. You have to accept the same.

Sometimes, I have to use a lot of antibacterial soap when I finish cleaning up, but I get through it. I complete the job. I don't begrudge anything I am called to do in the ministry, doing God's work. I wish I didn't have to do some things, but somebody's got to do them. And you have to be willing to do whatever it takes—whether that means taking out the trash, cleaning the toilets, or preaching to the congregation.

Nobody knows the price of the oil in my alabaster jar. Only you will know the price for you, but the reward is great. Whom do you want to please—God or man?

If you never get another accolade in your life, will you still be willing to serve the Lord? If you never get another "attaboy," will you be willing to serve the Lord? Are you looking for an "attaboy" from me or from somebody around you, or are you looking for an "attaboy" from God? He is telling you, "I have perfect confidence in you. My pride in you is full."

In this you greatly rejoice, though now for a little while, if need be, you have been grieved by various trials, that the genuineness of your faith, being much more precious than gold that perishes, though it is tested by fire, may be found to praise, honor, and glory at the revelation of Jesus Christ. (1 Peter 1:6–7)

Peter tells us that we will have trials and tribulations for a little while. We have to remember that it's for *"a little while."* When you go through a situation, you need to become the thermostat—not the thermometer. If all the people around you are belligerent and mad at you, don't adopt a negative attitude and say, "I'll show them. I'll just let them be sick." You are lowering yourself to their level. You are not reacting as Jesus would. Reset the thermostat.

If everybody around you is griping in a situation, how do you react? When you walk into a room, set the thermostat for a godly, loving environment, and it will become a godly, loving environment. The same principle applies to your home and business. As the head of your home, you can set the environment and end any backbiting and griping. As the head of a ministry, business, or department, you can control the thermostat by setting a precedent of *not* putting up with bad attitudes. Others around you need to rise to the level you have set as the standard.

Don't Give Up on the Anointing

Don't give up. Many, many people have encouraged me to throw in the towel throughout the years. They have told me, "You can't go through much more of this. You shouldn't have to go through any more stress. Just walk away from it." Some of these comments have come from people whom I have loved for years.

With no disrespect to them, I have had to say, "No, I can't walk away from the call of God on my life." I haven't given up, and I'm not planning on it. I thank God for everything that has happened to me, because those things have made me into a stronger person. I know that I have battles to fight and live through. I know that my path will not be on "Easy Street." With God's constant help and guidance, I will welcome the responsibility of leadership of the ministry to which He has called me.

You were custom-made for the call of God on your life. Are you welcoming that call? Are you preparing for what He is asking you to do? Are you open to His anointing? Are you truly willing?

I have a heart of compassion. I have giftings in the areas of healing the physical body and healing the heart. God told me, "Open the door for Me to win the hearts of people all over the world." When I go to England, they don't call me Joan Hunter, they call me "Joan of Hearts."

Do others think of you as a person "of hearts" or as a person "of hardened hearts"? What impression are you leaving with the people? Do you want an increase in pay? Do you want a promotion? Can your company go on without you? Everybody is dispensable. I am dispensable. However, I want to be important to God's work; I want to be valuable to His kingdom. I'm not talking about pride. I'm talking about my willingness to do whatever He wants me to do, at whatever cost He wants me to pay.

I remember when I first wanted to know more about His anointing. I got teaching tapes from Kenneth Hagin, Joyce Meyer, and Christian Harfouche. I was determined to learn everything there was to know about the anointing. I listened to one teaching after another. I prayed. I pondered. I listened to them all again and again. Step-by-step, I learned. There are many opinions or views on all subjects. The anointing was no different.

To create a salad, you add the greens, the vegetables, the oil and vinegar, the seasonings, some grated cheese, and maybe nuts, olives, grated eggs, or bacon bits. Many delicious tidbits are combined to create a tasty salad. I wanted to experience bits of what Kenneth Hagin experienced, a little bit of Joyce Meyer, a little bit of Christian Harfouche, a bit of this, and a little bit of that. Through a lot of prayer, study, and searching, all the ingredients combined to develop the delicious anointing that I walk in today.

I studied God's Word and read every Scripture on the anointing. I had watched my parents walk in it for years, and I wanted more. I was determined to learn what, where, and how it functioned. Did I learn it all? No, far from it. I am still searching, still learning, and still growing in what He has for me.

> *Honor the LORD with your possessions, and with the firstfruits of all your increase; so your barns will be filled with plenty, and your vats will overflow with new wine.* (Proverbs 3:9–10)

In order to walk in the anointing, it is vital for you to obey Him with your tithes and offerings. I am very much a proponent of giving to God. Do the fruits of all your increase include your birthday money? Yes. *"All your increase"* means *all*. Am I being legalistic? No. I'm saying that you have the privilege of giving to God. There's a big difference between "have to" and "get to." If you want to walk in the overflow of new wine, you need to honor Him with the firstfruits of all your increase. If He can't trust you to give your money when and as He directs, can He really trust you to give Him your life?

> *When I think of all this, I fall to my knees and pray to the Father, the Creator of everything in heaven and on earth. I pray that from his glorious, unlimited resources he will empower you with inner strength through his Spirit. Then Christ will make his home in your hearts as you trust in him. Your roots will grow down into God's love and keep you strong. And may you have the power to understand, as all God's people should, how wide, how long, how high, and how*

deep his love is. May you experience the love of Christ, though it is too great to understand fully. Then you will be made complete with all the fullness of life and power that comes from God.

(Ephesians 3:14–19 NLT)

The LORD replied, "Look around at the nations; look and be amazed! For I am doing something in your own day, something you wouldn't believe even if someone told you about it."   (Habakkuk 1:5 NLT)

Several years ago, a lady whom I've known for many, many years gave me a prophetic word from the Lord. She told me that she had actually argued with God before telling me: "God, are You sure? Is this the same Joan that both You and I know?" After about two weeks, God wouldn't release her from it, so she shared the word with me. I talked to her a few years later to let her know that everything she had prophesied had come to pass. I added, "And this is just the beginning."

The Word says that you are going to have a hard time believing in miracles if you don't see them. Each time I share some of the marvelous healings that we have seen around the world, I am totally amazed. God keeps on doing His thing, whether I comprehend His work or not. *"Blessed is she who believed, for there will be a fulfillment of those things which were told her from the Lord"* (Luke 1:45).

There are many, many Scriptures about the anointing. I could have ignored them. I could have run in the other direction, away from the ministry and from His anointing. However, instead of running away from the vision, I ran into the vision and embraced it. Now, it has become a part of me. Part of the vision that God has shown me has now become part of my memory. It is so exciting to know that there is more to come!

Why haven't all our dreams and visions come to pass? That is a very good question. God's timing may not be our timing, or the circumstances may not be right. We have to prepare ourselves. We have to be willing and believe that He can use us. We have to open our spirits to His Holy Spirit. We have to endeavor to walk in holiness and reject sin in our lives.

Listen to the Lord

If the Lord calls you to do something, He also provides what you need to complete the assignment. That may include finances, other people, open doors, or information. What you may need more than anything else, however, are His anointing, supernatural power, understanding, and wisdom. He anoints, He sends, and He provides. If you have accepted Him and His salvation by faith, you can also accept His anointing to do His work with that same measure of faith. Remember, we are designed to be His hands on earth.

If the Lord calls you to do something, He also provides what you need to complete the assignment.

Are you ready to allow Him to work through you? Is there sin keeping His anointing from flowing through you?

You were wearied by all your ways, but you would not say, "It is hopeless." You found renewal of your strength, and so you did not faint.
(Isaiah 57:10 NIV)

The passage above contains a key statement. It says that you strengthened *yourself*. You didn't give up; you went on. That's incredible. It doesn't say that another person came to strengthen you. You can do this. God may direct you to a person to assist you, just like He directed you to read this book. However, when you seek God, He can help you in ways that the words of man never can.

The people of Israel are saying, "He's talking about the distant future. His visions won't come true for a long, long time." Therefore, tell them, "This is what the Sovereign LORD says: No more delay! I will now do everything I have threatened. I, the Sovereign LORD, have spoken!"
(Ezekiel 12:27–28 NLT)

Have people been telling you that all of your dreams and visions are never going to come to pass? Do they tell you to forget about them? After examining your God-given dreams and visions, you must believe that the delay has ended. You must recognize that they will indeed come to pass.

I want to walk in all the anointing that God has for me. I want to walk in all the anointing that one person can actually have and still remain alive on this earth. There's another Scripture that is important to keep in mind as you do what God wants you to do and walk in the anointing.

> *"Now therefore, I pray, if I have found grace in Your sight, show me now Your way, that I may know You and that I may find grace in Your sight. And consider that this nation is Your people." And He said, "My Presence will go with you, and I will give you rest." Then he said to Him, "If Your Presence does not go with us, do not bring us up from here."* (Exodus 33:13–15)

If God doesn't direct you to go somewhere, wait.

In today's language, this means that if God doesn't direct you to go somewhere, *wait*. It is so important not to get ahead of God. I don't want to go anywhere if His presence doesn't go first.

"And he poured some of the anointing oil on Aaron's head and anointed him, to consecrate him" (Leviticus 8:12). Anointing and consecration go hand in hand. Anointing oil is symbolic of the Holy Spirit. Allow the Holy Spirit to come in and consecrate you, purifying you.

And they served drinks in golden vessels, each vessel being different from the other, with royal wine in abundance, according to the generosity of the king. In accordance with the law, the drinking was not compulsory; for so the king had ordered all the officers of his household, that they should do according to each man's pleasure. (Esther 1:7–8)

I believe that the anointing is available to everybody, but we need to be aware of the anointing and never *ever* take it lightly. The verse above says, *"they served drinks in golden vessels, each vessel being different from the other."* Think of someone you know. Are you different from him or her? Of course. Each person is created differently. We are all unique individuals who do not look exactly like any another person. Twins may be very similar, but even the most identical twins have their differences. Whether blond, brunette, short, tall, fat, or skinny, there is a huge diversity of people on this earth.

We are all vessels, and each vessel is different from the others. As written in Esther, the royal wine was given *"according to the generosity of the king."* In other words, God's anointing is given to us according to the generosity of our God. How generous is our God? My God is very generous. How about yours?

"With royal wine in abundance." There is an abundance of His anointing that He wants to give out. He will not withhold His anointing when we want it and ask for it. He desires to bless us in every way.

"In accordance with the law, the drinking was not compulsory." God will not force you to walk in the anointing. He will not give you more than you want.

"The king had ordered all the officers of his household … according to each man's pleasure." What do you want? How much do you want? What are you willing to pay to get it? What are you willing to do to walk in it?

The Anointing Is to Bless Others

The anointing is not for yourself. It is for others. It is not to make you look good or sound good. It is simply not for you. The anointing is the conduit through which God can use you and move through you. It is not a toy, and it is not to be played with; it's very serious. His anointing is to be guarded and treated with the utmost respect. Under it, you no longer live for yourself—you live for others.

> The anointing is not for yourself. It is for others.

213

As part of the ministry team, we say, "I no longer live for me, I live for You, Lord. I don't do this because I want to do the work of the ministry, but I lay down my life for the ministry."

Many times, as I have ministered to people on an individual basis during a service, they have received spiritual face-lifts. Our ministry team has been trained to minister to more than just physical needs. As I see lives changed as a result of God healing hearts, I stand in awe. Not pointing at any particular person, I have often stated, "I would do it all again for what I know now, just to set that one person free."

No matter what kind of situation I went through, no matter what kind of hell it was, God has allowed me to use every experience and turn it around for His glory and for His ministry—not for me, not for my glory. And that's one thing that is so neat about the ministry. I don't want to hear, "Praise Joan." It is always and forever, "Praise Jesus!"

I know I walk in the anointing; I know that God can heal through me because I have seen it happen day after day, year after year. Whether I'm on the phone at the office, on the road, or on an airplane, God uses me. And I want other people to recognize that God can use them, also.

Serving Him is a daily decision, almost moment by moment, situation after situation. If you want to walk in obedience to Him, you must choose whom you will serve every day of your life! It is your decision to serve Him. He will not force you. You must be willing.

Serving Him is not about you. It is about God getting all the glory. In services, you will hear us say that we just watch God answer prayer. When you minister to others, that is what you will be doing—watching. The sick and needy have been praying for God to heal them, and God just happens to use you. So, you will just watch God answer prayer.

So God can point to us in all future ages as examples of the incredible wealth of his grace and kindness toward us, as shown in all he has done for us who are united with Christ Jesus.

(Ephesians 2:7 NLT)

an example of His wealth and favor in every area of my life. I want to be an example to others.

What do you want from Him? How much do you want? Daily, God gives out of the abundance of His heart. His generosity cannot be measured. He is the King of kings, and He will give you as much as you want.

Are You Ready?

Do you want it? God can use you! Read, learn, and pray, and act. Obey His Word and His Holy Spirit. Allow the Spirit to work through you. Allow His anointing into every area of your life. It is amazing what He can do through His willing children. Notice that I said "willing." He has lots of unwilling children—those who believe in Him but don't want to do anything else for Him. They don't live within His perfect will or experience His abundant life.

> **Are you ready? Do you want it? God can use you!**

God gives different people different levels of anointing and gifts. I believe that I have received extra talents and gifts because of my parents and the inheritance I received through their faithfulness to God. However, because of my willingness and determination to walk in obedience, He has given me more. He has multiplied those gifts that He originally gave me. If we use our talents, God will multiply them. If we sit on them like quarterbacks quickly falling on footballs, our gifts will atrophy from lack of use, and He will bless someone else with those gifts. What have you done with yours?

Jesse Duplantis was thanking God one day for taking him around the world and allowing him to see what he had seen. In the small voice of the Holy Spirit, God told him, "Thank you for taking Me around the world!" This was an incredible revelation to me. Many times, I have thanked God for taking me around the world. And in turn, He is thanking me for taking Him around the world.

God wants to thank the people who are not only reading this book but are also learning more about Him and preparing to take Him and His healing power around the world to help people find healing—whether physically, mentally, or financially.

Some people try to catch the wave of what God is doing. Others make the wave. I want to speak to you who are reading this today. I speak this day that you are going to be a wave maker, not just a follower. God will raise you up to higher levels than you have ever dreamed of in the past. Take the limits off of God, and He will take the limits off of you.

Welcome Him! Welcome His Spirit! Welcome His anointing! Ask Him for more! There is nothing on earth more precious, more awesome than what He freely gives when we open our hearts totally to His anointing. Pray with me.

> Father, I want all of You. I want all You are willing to give me. I freely give You all areas of my life. I want Your Holy Spirit to work through me. Make me so sensitive to You and Your precious Holy Spirit that I walk obediently in Your perfect will every day and in every situation. Open my eyes, ears, and heart to the hurting people around me. Let me walk in the compassion of Jesus and be His hands as I reach out to help others. Anoint my hands to lay them on the sick so they will recover. Anoint my feet so they will go only in places where You want them to go. Father, set a fire in my soul. I want Holy Spirit boldness like I have never experienced before. Give me greater faith to do Your work and carry out the calling You have on my life, in Jesus' name. Amen.

Let's go! Let's take God and His anointing around the world!

Conclusion

It is my prayer that what you have read in this book has ministered to you where you needed it most. As I travel around the world, I see people's lives transformed through the things God has shown me, either directly or indirectly. I'm thankful not just because I know these things, but because I can share them with others. God doesn't want it to stop here. He wants the world to be healed, especially His children.

The enemy and the hardships of life have taken so much joy from so many people, and many of them have just left it at that. I want you to receive back *all* that the enemy has stolen—time, money, relationships, love, joy, and health. In applying the principles in this book, you can walk out the road of restoration and healing—not only for yourself, but for others, as well.

A friend of mine, John Paul Jackson, is known for dream interpretation and for teaching others how to interpret dreams. When he interpreted a certain dream many years ago, some were amazed and asked him how he did it. "It was God," he responded. This happened over and over again—he gave God all the glory for the gift.

During the writing of this book, I went to a service with John, and he said something that burned into my heart. He told me that one day, through the Holy Spirit, God spoke to him and said, "Yes, I have given this gift to you, and you know how to do it. When you die, this gift will die with you, or you can share what I have taught you. I want others to know what you know." In the same way, God has given me this revelation. It is not to die with me, but it is for you to learn, go, and do!

God wants us to be *whole*—not just healed, but *whole*. During the bad times in my life, I could have chosen to stay where I was and die—mentally, spiritually, financially, and emotionally—*but I didn't!* I had to choose to get up, let go of pain, unforgiveness, poverty, illness, and stress, and let God do what He wanted to do.

I have learned so much from traveling with my parents, Charles and Frances Hunter, for more than thirty years of my life. I have seen so much, but I also had to pick up the mantle and go with it. God is not going to make us do anything we don't want to, no matter how good it would be for us.

It is up to you to pick up the mantle of healing and run with it. God is not going to make you pray for everyone around you. He is not going to make you prophesy over everyone. You *get* to!

As you move forth into the world, your eyes will be opened to those around you in need of healing, ministry, a hug, a smile, or just a word. God is going to send you right to the people who need *Him*. It is an exciting time to be used of God.

Go forth and be a blessing to all you meet!

About the Author

Joan Hunter has been involved in the healing ministry for over thirty years. Along with her parents, Charles and Frances Hunter, she has ministered to thousands of people in the area of physical healings. She has traveled the world, laying hands on the sick and seeing them recover. God has expanded her ministry to include total healing—body, soul, and spirit.

Joan is married to Kelley Murrell and lives in Pinehurst, Texas. She has four grown daughters, her husband has four sons, and she is a grandmother. She copastored a church in Dallas for eighteen years until 1999, giving her a wide range of experience in the ministry. She is also the author of *Healing the Heart* and *Healing the Whole Man Handbook*.

God has healed Joan in every area of her life. She encourages others that they can lay hands on the sick and see them recover. The healing power of God is not reserved for just a few but for all those who believe. Joan encourages you not to give up on your dreams and visions but to fulfill the destiny that God has for you.

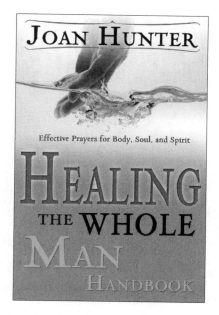

Healing the Whole Man Handbook
Joan Hunter

You can walk in divine health and healing. The secrets to God's words for healing and recovery are in this comprehensive, easy-to-follow guidebook containing powerful healing prayers that cover everything from abuse to yeast infections and everything in between. Truly anointed with the gifts of healing, Joan Hunter has over thirty years of experience praying for the sick and brokenhearted and seeing them healed and set free. By following these step-by-step instructions and claiming God's promises, you can be healed, set free, and made totally whole—body, soul, and spirit!

ISBN: 978-0-88368-815-8 ♦ Trade ♦ 240 pages

WHITAKER
HOUSE

Healing the Heart
Joan Hunter

For anyone who has ever been betrayed...
For anyone who has ever felt lost, abused, or abandoned...
For anyone who has ever suffered a broken heart...
THERE IS HEALING!

In this inspiring and life-changing book, Joan Hunter shares her challenging testimony of how she overcame rejection and the worst betrayal imaginable. No matter what your circumstances, God wants to minister to you through Joan's insights and practical advice. On the cross, Jesus paid for more than your physical healing. He has also made provision for *Healing the Heart.*

ISBN: 978-0-88368-130-5 ◆ Trade ◆ 192 pages

WHITAKER
HOUSE

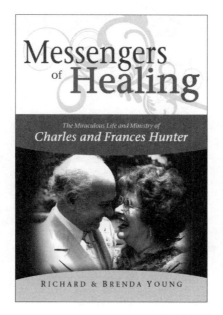

Messengers of Healing
Richard and Brenda Young

Charles and Frances Hunter are nationally recognized both
for their powerful healing ministry and for their unbridled,
contagious joy. What few people know, however, is that Frances
spent years as a "wild sinner," and Charles was a "dried-up
spiritual prune" for most of his early life. As you follow the
Hunters' incredible journeys, you will see how ordinary people
are impacting the world as a direct result of yielding to God and
learn how you can impact your world, too!

ISBN: 978-1-60374-106-4 • Trade • 208 pages

WHITAKER
HOUSE

How to Heal the Sick
Charles and Frances Hunter

A loved one is sick…your friend was just in an accident…a family member is facing an emotional crisis. Have you ever desperately longed to reach out your hand and bring healing to these needs? At times our hearts ache with the desire to help, but either we don't know how or we are afraid and stop short. The truth is that, as a Christian, the Holy Spirit within you is ready to heal the sick! Charles and Frances Hunter present solid, biblically based methods of healing that can bring not only physical health, but also spiritual wholeness and the abundant life to you, your family, and everyone around you.

ISBN: 978-0-88368-600-3 ◆ Trade ◆ 224 pages

WHITAKER
HOUSE